T0077480

MALIBONGWE

Malibongwe

EDITED BY SONO MOLEFE

WITH A NEW PREFACE BY UHURU PHALAFALA
AND A NEW INTRODUCTION BY MAKHOSAZANA XABA

UHLANGA
2020

Malibongwe

Edited by Sono Molefe

All poems © the authors, 1981, all rights reserved
Selection of poems and foreword © Lindiwe Mabuza, 1981, 2020, all rights reserved
Preface © Uhuru Phalafala, 2020, all rights reserved
Introduction © Makhosazana Xaba, 2020, all rights reserved

ISBN: 978-0-620-86912-6

First South African edition published in Durban in 2020 by uHlanga
UHLANGAPRESS.CO.ZA

This edition distributed outside of South Africa by the African Books Collective
AFRICANBOOKSCOLLECTIVE.COM

Support for the publication of this book was furnished by
THE ANDREW W. MELLON FOUNDATION

This collection first published in English in 1981 as *Malibongwe: ANC Women:
Poetry is also their Weapon* by Sono Molefe/African National Congress, with the support of
the Arbetarrörelsens Internationella Centrum and the Kooperativa Gillesförbundet, Sweden

This edition carries minor grammatical edits to the 1981 edition

Designed and typeset by Nick Mulgrew
Proofread by Karina Szczurek and Jennifer Jacobs

Cover art by Dumile Feni, "Untitled", courtesy of the Dumile Feni Estate,
first published in 1987 in *Malibongwe: Gedichte südafrikanischer Frauen*
by Weltkreis/Pahl-Rugenstein Verlag, Cologne, Federal Republic of Germany

Royalties from this publication will be donated to the Oliver and Adelaide Tambo Foundation

CONTENTS

CONTENTS *CONTINUED*

PHASES OF STRUGGLE: RESOLUTION, EXILE, PERSPECTIVE, LOVE, CALL TO JUSTICE AND ARMS

PREFACE: TENDING OUR MOTHERS' GARDEN

Uhuru Phalafala

I HAVE BEEN teaching a course on Black Consciousness poetry in universities for close to seven years and have been nagged by the silence and absence of women in that unfolding radical moment.

For about five years now, every August, the month in which South Africa marks Women's Month, an image from the 1980s of Minister Lindiwe Zulu circulates on social media. She looks away from the book in her hands to confront us with a direct gaze, a Kalashnikov resting easily next to her hip. The image represents a battle fought with both ideological and military warfare; what the Cold War machine would have called soft power (culture) and hard power (artillery). That image of a female guerilla looks as provocative as it does organic: the people closest to the pain should be closest to power, driving and informing the contours and contents of a revolution. The country's history dictated its constitution: black, hypermasculine, clandestine, and Molotov-wielding. The battle lines were drawn along racial lines exclusively. When the white oligarchy peddled fear in their white subjects through the image of swartgevaar, what they conjured was not black women. But history absolves them today. Their variegated voices, erased by national liberation narratives, shall be heard. Black women were at the frontlines. In the underground they were confronted with a distinctive battle, against both the white supremacist machine impaling their families and communities, and against hetero-patriarchy within their ranks. To be a female guerrilla was to submit oneself to multiple warfares. They were in the trenches of Tanzania, Angola, and Mozambique as fighters, teachers, students, guerillas, and nurses.

It was in this context that Lindiwe Mabuza championed the *Malibongwe* book project. She drafted a letter to head of the ANC Women's Section, Florence Maphosho, to propose the idea. Mabuza asked Maphosho to disseminate the letter to all the women in the camps, offices of the ANC around the world, and at the nascent Solomon Mahlangu Freedom College (SOMAFCO) in Tanzania. There was great interest: hand-written submissions from all the camps began to arrive in Lusaka. Angela Dladla-Sangweni, Mabuza's sister-in-law, helped to type all the poems. Mabuza had the full manuscript by the time she went to Sweden in 1979. At the time she was also at the helm of fundraising to construct the new SOMAFCO, and had arranged for artists within the Angola camps to contribute drawings and illustrations which she could sell to advance that cause. She sold the originals in several Scandinavian countries, as she was ANC's official representative to the entire Nordic region, but kept copies for inclusion in *Malibongwe*'s first English edition. She approached the then-secretary at the Center for International Solidarity in Sweden, Bjorn Andreasson, to help with funding the publication of the poetry anthology. While this was in the pipeline, a German translation became the first version of *Malibongwe* to be published, by Munich-based Weltkreis-Verlag in 1980. Translated by Peter Schütt, this edition was expedited by the ambassador of the ANC Mission for the Federal Republic of Germany and Austria, Tony Seedat, and wife, Dr Aziza Seedat. They had already been in liaison with the publisher in 1980, who was at the time publishing another South African poetry collection by Keorapetse Kgositsile titled *Herzspeuren* (*Heartprints*), at the behest of Aziza Seedat.

In 1981, Bengt Säve-Söderbergh of the Centre for International Solidarity of the Labour Organisation in Sweden had taken over the full publication process, and published 2 000 English language copies of *Malibongwe*. Most copies were distributed by ANC officials around the world, at the discretion of the party's Chief Representatives. At subsequent ANC meetings and rallies, people were reading the women's poetry. Meanwhile, Säve-Söderbergh approved funding for Erik Stinus to translate the anthology into Swedish and Danish, copies of which were published in 1982 by the anti-apartheid solidarity group Mellemfolkeligt Samvirke. Later in the 1980s, the Finnish Peace Committee translated and published a small run of the anthology in Helsinki. The demand for *Malibongwe*'s

German version resulted in a second edition being reprinted in 1987. Inspired by the illustration and design of Kgositsile's collection, this edition carried illustrations by ANC member and eminent abstract expressionist Dumile Feni, including one on its cover. These networks of international solidarity and support attest to the power of culture in fostering the political tools of revolution. By reprinting one of Feni's awe-inspiring pieces on the cover of this edition, we carry on this spirit of collaboration.

Some of the poets in this anthology have used pseudonyms as they were underground. The editor Lindiwe Mabuza is listed as Sono Molefe. She has provided a list of confirmed birth names of some contributors: Gloria Mntungwa's birth name is Belinda Martins; Jumaimah Mutaung is Yvonne Modiagotle; Lerato Kumalo is S'bongile Mvubelo; Rebecca Matlou is Sanki Mthembi-Mahanyele; Alice Tsongo is Phumza Dyanti; Mpho Maruping is Mpho Msimang; Susan Lamu is Ribbon Mosholi; Baleka Kgositsile is now Baleka Mbete; and Duduzile Ndelu is Thuli Kubeka. Say their names and afford them their place in literary and political history! The following contributors have since passed on: Belinda Martins, Thuli Kubeka, Phumzile Zulu, and Mpho Segomotso Dombo. May their revolutionary souls rest in peace.

Decades later, in the dispensation for which they sacrificed their lives, their work is virtually unknown, out of print and circulation. The absence was loud for I knew deep in my bones that as long as there were women fighting in uMkhonto we Sizwe, there had to be women writing poetry that encapsulated the moment. I initiated a project titled 'Recovering Subterranean Archives', the main objective of which was to research into South African culture in exile. It was a logical step in the face of a missing national archive. The pursuit of such a rich record would have to entail interviews and physical tracking of the ANC's activities.

I came to know of *Malibongwe* through my personal project on the towering figure of Keorapetse Kgositsile – statesman, former national poet laureate, and academic. I had previously seen the poetry of ANC women in exile interspersed with that of their male comrades, published in the anthology *Somehow We Survive* (1982), which Kgositsile had assembled and sent to the New York publisher, Thunder's Mouth Press. This piqued my curiosity on whether there was not a full-length anthology of their poetry elsewhere. He revealed to me the anthology whose second English edition you now hold in your hands. The sense of urgency was acute in getting this book republished, to change the narrative of women's involvement in the cultural war against apartheid and in the black liberation movement.

Through the Andrew W. Mellon Foundation I was able to secure the funds to reproduce this important text against all odds related to rights. Nick Mulgrew of uHlanga stepped up and investigated the genesis of the book, secured me an interview with Dr Lindiwe Mabuza, and motioned the process forward. I am grateful to Makhosazana Xaba for weaving a brilliant and timely introduction, and am proud to be able to tend to the seeds that our mothers planted for us. Thank you too to my colleague Dr Wamuwi Mbao, as well as the participants of the January 2019 colloquium on the repatriation of South African culture from exile. Finally, thank you to Marriam Diale, daughter of Dumile Feni and representative of his Estate, for permission to reprint her father's work.

May this book contribute to the deep listening of our elders' struggles, and may it give us courage to fulfil to our own generation's mission.

CAPE TOWN, 2020

INTRODUCTION

MAKHOSAZANA XABA

"WHAT DOES IT mean to giggle at the wrinkled hands that pried open bolted doors so we could walk in and take a seat at the table?" Grace A. Musila, a literary scholar with interests in (among others) gender studies, the African intellectual archive, and postcolonial whiteness, raised the above question in a recent article about the contribution made by post-colonial theorists – those who "fought the epistemic injustice of canon-ising certain literature over others" – to our current times. Grace's question is pertinent and timely, and shouldn't be limited to being asked of postcolonial theorists. The South African edition of *Malibongwe* – com-piled and edited by Sono Molefe, a.k.a. Lindiwe Mabuza – excavates the names of poets whose wrinkled hands contemporary Black women po-ets need to know about and then acknowledge whichever way they see fit. Some might want to shake their hands in gratitude. Others might wish to hold hands, just as a way to connect. Some might want to buy some moisturising hand cream and offer it. Hopefully none will giggle.

Giggling at the poets and poetry borne of what the foreword to the orig-inal edition called "a love deeply rooted in their usurped land" would con-stitute a failure to recognise their significance. To return to Grace:

> One thing Black women artists have taught us is the importance
> of acknowledging our intellectual histories and those who dreamt
> the futures we enjoy, and our responsibility to dream more live-
> able futures for those behind us.

While living in exile I knew about the existence of *Malibongwe*, but I never held a copy in my hands. It was only in the late 1980s that I met Lindiwe, as well as three of the book's contributors, Baleka Kgositsile, Ilva Mackay and Rebecca Matlou. While I lived in Lusaka, Zambia, I shared a communal African National Congress (ANC) home in Chilenje with Rebecca, while Baleka lived close by, no more than a ten minute walk away. Eventually I learned that the two of them were poets. Later, I learned that Lindiwe and Ilva were also poets. I never came across their work while in exile.

What I do know is that these poets – or these hands, to return to Musila's metaphor – pried open bolted doors so I could walk in and claim a chair around the literary table, even though I never wrote a single poem while living and moving within the ANC spaces and places in exile. These poets' multiple identities as comrades spanned from being activists to ambassadors (Chief Representatives as we called them, pre-1990), as well as combatants, feminists, guerillas, mothers, public intellectuals, scholars, sisters, wives, writers, and more.

For this anthology, I wish to call them comrades-cum-poets. These poets are, for me, living examples of the ever-expanding range of identities we can claim, as women. Although I have loved and enjoyed poetry all my life, it was only in 2000 that I began to claim it and write. It became an easy transition because in my earlier life I had known Black women who were poets. To finally place my hands on the *Malibongwe* manuscript makes me want to say: Malibongwe indeed!

Malibongwe is an anthology of sixty poems with contributions from nineteen poets including one who chose to stay anonymous. Choosing to be anonymous in that time was of course about safety and security. Lindiwe also uses a pen name, Sono Molefe, as both editor of the anthology and author of "We demand punishment", its last poem. Coincidentally, the four poets I met in Lusaka each contributed the most poems: Lindiwe eleven (twelve, counting the one written as Sono Molefe), Baleka eight, Rebecca seven, and Ilva five.

Unsurprisingly, although there are many contributors, *Malibongwe* speaks as a collective voice. To illustrate, I have chosen some words from Lindiwe-as-Sono-Molefe's foreword to the original anthology:

We shall be free

"We shall be free"
Is the tough fibre that binds.
Who are these women?
They are no striking personalities individually.

There is no romance here, all attest
a love rooted in their usurped land
No academic optimism
No unwarned pessimism
Only pounding reality
Now unpalatable – now lifting
Always moving towards the ultimate success

This collective voice:
People you can hear and know.
Find them: discover some peculiarities
Then love the harmony of song.

Pounding reality. Pounding. Reality pounding. Reality. How do we understand this pounding reality of the now-wrinkled hands that pried open bolted doors? Where are they? How would they speak about their hands today? It is encouraging to know that these once-bolted doors are now open and the tables have empty chairs to sit on. Even though the conversations may be divisive, heated, infuriating, insulting and patronising (and others even stage walk-outs), a reconvening can be organised. A return to the table is always a possibility. There are no more bolted doors! What does it mean then to return to an anthology birthed during a period of bolted doors? What is the texture of today's reality? What is the rhythm of its pounding? What does today's pounding reality look, feel and taste like? What sound does it make? What does it mean to engage with it? What continuities does the engaging unearth?

FIRST, SOME WORDS about *Malibongwe*'s composition. There are six sections in the anthology: "Africa shall be free", "Birth and genocide", "Spirit of Soweto: the ghetto, massacres, resolve", "Women in struggle", "Our men who fought and died and fight", and "Phases of struggle: resolution, exile, perspective, love, call to justice and arms". Many of these themes remain as relevant in South Africa today as they were in the past, similar to how the inhumanity of the apartheid regime translated into inhumanities perpetuated by democratic regime. (Perhaps best exemplified by the Life Healthcare Esidimeni saga, in which more than 140 psychiatric patients in Gauteng died of starvation and neglect after the provincial Department of Health removed them from care.)

But while the themes carry over from the old to the new, specific examples do not always. Throughout *Malibongwe*, the poets honour prominent comrades, women who were imprisoned, executed, bombed or killed. Names of the women honoured by the poets in *Malibongwe* are Charlotte Maxeke, Dorothy Nyembe, Esther ka-Maleka, Helen Joseph, Lilian Ngoyi, Mary Moodley, and Paulina Mogale. My curiousity heightens whenever I come across the name of a woman who contributed to the struggle that I have never heard of, and invariably a research journey begins. This is my commitment to "self-education", one I have seen as necessary in a country where women's contributions to society are valued less than those of men, which often means that their names disappear. I had never heard of Esther ka-Maleka and Paulina Mogale until I read *Malibongwe*. These are, in the words of Mpho Maruping in her poem "To our mothers!", women on whose steps we need to tread.

There are fewer poems in "Women in struggle" than in the next section, which is devoted to men in the struggle. In an anthology by women I expected to see more poems about women specifically. That said, we also know that the apartheid regime targeted men consistently because of their visibility and their embodiment of what the apartheid regime considered to be the "swart-gevaar." With this in mind – as well as the understanding of poetry's propensity for speaking to, pointing out and denouncing the gross, the extreme, the most painful – I do understand why women wrote more poems about men.

WITH A BOOK like this, it is important to put the past and present in conversation. A number of researchers have published work on *Malibongwe* before this new edition. In 1992, the researcher Lynda Gilfillan published an article entitled "Black Women Poets in Exile: The Weapon of Words", in which she analysed some of the poems in *Malibongwe*. She highlighted some poets for praise, and offered others literary critiques. She also discussed "lacks", "avoidances", "gaps" and "silences", but pointed out that "The *Malibongwe* poets produced a particular cultural artefact at a specific historical conjuncture. The circumstances surrounding the production and publication of *Malibongwe* should therefore be taken into account" (88). Although I recommend a reading of this article in full, it's worth considering its final paragraph in particular:

> Black women may yet write poetry that is a weapon in a broader
> liberation struggle. The "warrior women" poets of the past may
> even become legislators in a future South Africa from which the
> father figure as well as a nation state have been exorcised. If so,
> they may then find that while words are effective literary weapons,
> they may also be used to weave. (89)

As I will revisit later, I would argue that, in fact, these warrior women achieved both: words were their weapons, but they were also what they weaved with to create artifacts of *both* political and literary value. As early as 1990 the Congress of South African Writers published the first collection of poetry by Rebecca Matlou (a.k.a. Sankie Dolly Nkondo, a.k.a. Sankie Mthembi-Mahanyele), *Flames of Fury and other Poems*, in which four poems ("Solomon

Mahlangu", "A Gulp of Unity", "Swim Comrade" and "Oliver Waka Tambo") also appear in *Malibongwe*. In his introduction to this collection Patrick Wilmot writes that the author, "a poet and militant",

> is aware of the dual requirements of artistic form and political content. The poems are finely crafted, economical, fluid, imaginative. The images flow smoothly in articulate and coherent patterns of meaning. (5)

The political and the literary are not mutually exclusive, and should not be treated as such. The current agenda to rebuild South Africa is a familiar one, recently revisited, that focuses on the emotional healing of wounds inflicted by a systematically violent apartheid regime. This agenda greatly distances the conversations South Africans need to have about exorcising their nation state and its father figures. Truth and reconciliation were mere starting points of a process that has not yet finished. We are yet to see justice for crimes committed during the apartheid years.

Gloria Vangile Kgalane's masters dissertation entitled "Black South African Women's Poetry (1970–1991): A Critical Survey" has a chapter dedicated to poetry produced by Black women in exile. I recommend this dissertation highly, not least because it contextualises *Malibongwe* at many levels, as well as analysing it. In this analysis, Gloria identifies the poetry of Phyllis Altman and Lindiwe Mabuza in particular as "self-consciously 'feminist'", which "sets them apart from the more conventional 'liberation poetry'" (133). I agree, but I wish to add that *Malibongwe* as a whole is a feminist *book project*. In an essay I wrote for *Our Words, Our Worlds: Writing on Black South African Women Poets, 2000-2018*, I made the point that

> The physicality of the book is an enactment of presence, a claim to visibility and an invitation to engagement. It is also useful for periodisation, quantification and analysis. The concreteness of a book therefore reduces the probability of erasure while mitigating against denial. (40)

Malibongwe made visible women's voices and ideas as literary contributions within a context that made visible and valued men more than it did women. It disrupted a patriarchal norm. Implicit in this is an understanding of women's multiple identities, beyond the narrow ones that are accepted and normalised by the ideology of hetero-patriarchy. In *Malibongwe's* original sub-title, "Poetry is also their weapon", their identities as creative literary individuals are affirmed, confirmed and normalised. Of course, it is true that not all the contributors identify or identified as poets – writing poems does not automatically make a person a "poet"; nevertheless, thanks to *Malibongwe*, their contributions are now available for analysis and critique.

This then is the added significance of the return of *Malibongwe*, in its first South African edition. As the curiosity grows about and interest in the lives of South African former exiles, *Malibongwe* is a living archive that can be accessed with ease. It provides evidence of discernable meeting points between the past and the present. For instance, in the preface to this current edition, Uhuru Phalafala tells the story behind the concept and production of *Malibongwe,* personified in Lindiwe's leadership as an editor. It is a story of a specific historical conjuncture. The story unfolds in the telling of subsequent reprints and translated editions; a laudable testament to Lindiwe's passion as a feminist writer and curator. Her published poetry collections – *From ANC to Sweden* (1987), *Letter to Letta* (1991), *Voices that Lead: Poems 1976–1996* (1998), *Africa to Me* (1998), and *Footprints and Fingerprints* (2008) – are collective testament to her passion for poetry and her prolific contributions to literature. Her recent lifetime awards – the 2017 Lifetime Achievement Award for Arts Advocacy and the 2014 National Order of Ikhamanga, for her contribution towards the eradication of the oppressive apartheid system through the arts – make her legacy indelible, particularly as some of her poetry collections are now out of print. Lindiwe's work and legacy in the cultural sphere is a story we need to be able to tell with ease. The archives of her international diplomacy work may be alive in the countries where she served, but hopefully *Malibongwe* inspires us to ensure that her work is archived and accessible in the country of her birth, a country she had to leave in order to fight for it.

Malibongwe is like a child born in exile to struggle parents. After decades of living in exile, it is finally a returnee. Through its publication in South Africa it has now come back home, to claim space and live. Notably, like other literary and cultural projects and products associated with liberation movements in South Africa, some of them have continued to live inaccessible and often isolated lives in exile, usually in the archives of organisations that were part of the Anti-Apartheid Movement (AAM) internationally. I remember clearly in 2002 watching a documentary film, *Amandla!: A Revolution in Four-Part Harmony*, and wondering just how many South Africans had access to it. I remember wondering how many South Africans knew of the use of music by ordinary ANC activists who were part of the musical group Amandla Cultural Ensemble that toured many countries of the world. These ANC activists did not have the kind of prominence that the likes of Miriam Makeba, Jonas Gwangwa and Hugh Masekela had. Like the majority of the poets contributing to *Malibongwe,* these comrades were no striking personalities individually. They were held together by the glue of their commitment to the struggle. Where is the story of Amandla Cultural Ensemble being kept? How accessible is it? What is to be learned from the experiences of this group? Was their music also their weapon?

In *Malibongwe* we witness how our past also resides in our present. We confirm yet again that history repeats itself. In Lindiwe's poem of just over twenty stanzas on the founding of the ANC at Mangaung, the speaker proclaims that "I was born / At the gathering of the brave". This speaker could well be a member of the Congress of the People (COPE), a party founded by disgruntled members of the ANC in 2008. They were brave, the odds high against them. The speaker could also be a member of the Economic Freedom Fighters (EFF), founded by disgruntled members of the ANC Youth League in 2013. By then, the ANC was a century and one year old. They too were brave to stand apart.

Look too to the national #TotalShutdown of August 2018, where there were many gatherings of the brave, simultaneously, in many spots in the country, when the intersectional women's movement stood in protest against gender-based violence. Or to September 2019, when brave women gathered for the #SandtonShutdown, outside the Johannesburg Stock Exchange, the most visible representation of the intensity of capitalism in South Africa, to protest against gender-based and xenophobic violence. Each gathering of the brave births change.

In *Malibongwe* we read poems on the inhumanity of the apartheid's institutionalised racism, yet the questions asked of that government may be asked of the current democratic government. The promises we pinned on a post-apartheid, constitution-grounded democracy have been falling from the tree of hope like rotting fruit. See the exposure of a deep-rooted and widespread corruption within state-owned enterprises, or the 2012 Marikana Massacre of protesting miners by members of the South African police force, or more generally the pounding reality of gender-based violence, which leaves us wondering whether South African men have any humanity at all.

The republication of *Malibongwe* in 2020 thus becomes a mirror-holding exercise for South Africans. Holding the mirror we must ask the question and delve into the answers to the question – in the words of Mongane Wally Serote, quoted on the back cover of Lindiwe's collection *Footprints and Fingerprints* – of what we need to do "to be a little more humane". This question needs to become the rhythm of our daily lives.

I RETURN NOW to Lynda Gilfillan's reference to words being used as both weapon and weaving. The significance of *Malibongwe* as an excavation, or as a political and feminist project, does not only lie in its context or content, but also in its aesthetics. Accepting as I do just how deeply mired in controversy discussions about aesthetics can be sometimes, I cannot but share a few examples of what I consider to be exquisite writing in some of the poems, starting with the last two stanzas of the poem that opens the anthology, "Masechaba" by Ilva Mackay:

> Africa
> the voice of your children
> erodes the mist-shrouded mountains

like hungry rain
and cuts through the valleys
like pounding rivers that
that ravage and rape your fields

Africa
today your rivers heal our wounds
your fields offer us refuge
and your mountains do not silence, no they hold and harbour
the sounds of warriors answering the call for justice.

In this poem the spectacle of war and struggle are held inside the container of the African landscape. The container encloses them. They are almost hidden. Nature assumes the role of a holding, nurturing, comforting and safe fort and the health-giving rivers take on different roles. Whereas in the final stanza Africa's rivers heal, in the stanza before they pound, ravage and rape. The poem builds momentum delicately from the opening to the end, all the while grounded, literally, by the land, the sea, the rivers. It is a poem of hope, a vision of a future continent that nurtures and heals its inhabitants. It is an example of what Njabulo Ndebele argued for in his famous essay "The Rediscovery of the Ordinary", moving away from

a society of posturing and sloganeering; one that frowns upon *subtlety of thought and feeling and never permits the sobering power of contemplation*, of close analysis, and the *mature acceptance of failure,* weakness and limitation. (42, my emphasis)

"Masechaba", for me, is an embrace (and illustration) of the sobering power of contemplation, and the mature acceptance of failure, which moves toward resolution: Africa is a "mother of children / destitute / dying", but nevertheless "determined / to prescribe themselves freedom / to describe themselves free." The political is still identifiable and audible in ordinary visions of nature. Africa becomes merely a name, a geographical marker, not the hyperbolically romanticised entity of a continent we so love and will die for. We therefore are invited to engage levelheadedly with its content while at one with the flow and rhythm of nature.

For a second example, read Baleka Kgositsile's poem "Umkhonto":

> rhythm
> this dance is our future
> moving with the clumsy
> or graceful vigour of the present
> to the song of today
> echoed in our tomorrow
> rhythm
> we are all artists
> on this stage
> there is no break
> to this dance

This nine-stanza poem is intensely political in how it advocates for violence as part of the struggle for liberation. Yet also we read about rhythm and dance as propellers of the same struggle. Here, we find a subtlety of thought and feeling that Ndebele encourages. The commitment to the armed struggle is like that of artists on a stage; soldiers are prepared to die as simply as performers are prepared to dance. I hope Ndebele smiles.

In a third and last example on aesthetics I share the four lines that end Rebecca Matlou's poem "Solomon Mahlangu":

> bow to fate
> hold its quivering tale
> (to you I say)
> I touch this darkness and give it meaning

A posturing and sloganeering poet may have just used Solomon Mahlangu's often-quoted last words: "My blood will nourish the tree that will bear the fruits of freedom". But Rebecca's savvy has her use other words, "I touch this darkness and give it meaning". How much more understated can one be about an execution by the apartheid regime?

In these three examples, published in *Malibongwe* decades ago, it is clear that the poets were deliberate in their writerly craft. They weaved words to make poignant connections that were political, yes, but expressed with subtlety. The spectacle that was apartheid – even though it is the inspiration behind the poetry – recedes to the background and stays there. Artistic pleasure takes on centre stage. As we breathe, poetry becomes our oxygen.

I WISH TO discuss two themes visited upon in *Malibongwe* because of their renewed urgency in our current politics. The first theme is hope as expressed in the metaphor of dawn. The second is land.

When President Cyril Ramaphosa gave his State of the Nation address in 2018, his promise of a "new dawn" became a talking point. When public conversations and debates about accountability of government take place, this new dawn is often the most readily evoked expression because dawn is about new beginnings and is therefore promissory. Numerous poems in *Malibongwe* evoke hope despite the pounding reality of apartheid's crimes against humanity. In these poems we see a varying range of the usage of dawn as a metaphor:

> When the streets and rivers of our land turn red
> it will be the dawn of the day
> our land will kiss freedom welcome
>
> *From "For my unborn child" by Baleka Kgosistile*

The dawn of a dark day
Misery's spouse
The crying baby's body
Hangs on the light scales
of Kwashiokor

From "One life lost" by Jumaimah Motaung

Many seeking the light
Have fallen before their dawn
And I must go

From "I must go: Do not mourn" by Fezeka Makonese

With new dawn's energy
I must strengthen my sinews
For I have seen creatures stampede
And build icebergs in Liberty's path
But volcanic tides will charge
Making love to our own ploughs
Which must furrow for life

From "Soweto wishes" by Lindiwe Mabuza

What is it today, what was yesterday
shall tomorrow dawn to set for them?
Who ever prophesied this black cloud
this stiletto tear all of her here apart

From "Mother patriot (June 16, 1976 Soweto)"
by Rebecca Matlou

for you and I met
and always will
to forge multiple dawns
of new horizons

From "To a comrade" by Lindiwe Mabuza

The numerous ways in which dawn is used re-iterates the point that the past lives in the present. We see the continuity in "and always will". We see the broadness of the scope of work that needs to be done in "to forge multiple dawns". And we see the boundaries being pushed farther and farther in "of new horizons". Decades ago, Lindiwe Mabuza was suggesting that the change we want is in our hands and it is at many levels, on numerous fronts.

The second theme, land, also abounds in *Malibongwe*. In 2018 we witnessed a nationwide solicitation of views from the public on whether Section 25 of the Constitution of 1996 should be amended to include the expropriation of land without compensation, and the topic became the centre of many heated and appropriately emotional debates. Five years earlier nationwide events had focused on remembering the 1913 Land Act and its devastating effects on the lives of Black people. As Baleka Kgositsile says in her poem, "Umkhonto",

Yes
our today's dance
towards a better tomorrow
is dictated by yesterday

The "stench of colonialism", as Baleka calls it in the same poem, will forever spoil the air we breathe for as long as the land question is not resolved to the satisfaction of Black people who were dispossessed. Many of the poets in *Malibongwe* refer to land directly, indirectly, tangentially and implicitly. Sometimes land is evoked in intensely emotional ways that make us revisit and thus rediscover the ordinary, Ndebele-esque, as in Fezeka Makonese's "I must go: Do not mourn":

These roses and other flowers
In your garden urge me to go
They evoke memories of wreaths

Memories of wreaths. Wreaths are markers of land. Wreaths signify death's pounding reality. If Fezeka were a posturing and sloganeering writer her focus would have been on the spectacle that was the oppressors who are the causes of these deaths she was referring to. To use Ndebele's words, Fezeka would have focused on the "massively demonstrated horror that has gone before" (38). Instead, she weaves words as she focuses on the subtlety of thought and feeling. She evokes a wreath, which says: land, flower, nature's beauty, the circle of life. The interiority evoked by Fezeka is soft, personal, engaging and tenderly emotional. When the horror that has gone before, is palpable in "urge me to go", these four short words deliver a clear decision, while we sit with contemplation upon roses and flowers, in the garden. We sit with art rather than politics. And so again, we breathe.

LET ME END with the poem of over thirty stanzas that ends *Malibongwe*, "We demand punishment", written by the editor Sono Molefe (a.k.a. Lindiwe Mabuza) which she dedicates to the poet Pablo Neruda. This poem is many things: a lesson in histories, a fingering of criminal acts from the colonial to the apartheid era, a demand for justice. Most importantly, it is about the justice we needed then and continue to need now.

> Ovens of terror unleash their flames
> when orders to shoot to kill rampage our land

> Remember Marikana?

> They say kaffirs make good manure
> when they murder us

Today we could change one word "kaffirs" to "women" and the poem's sentiment would be same. The statistics are our witnesses.

We demand punishment on top of the forgiveness and reconciliation. We demand punishment of all the perpetrators of crimes against women and children. We demand punishment of all the criminals implicated in corruption. Punishment is justice, the poem suggests, and, it is our right to continue to demand it.

One of the main differences between the apartheid era and the post-1994 era is that the enemy was easy to point out. Lines have since been blurred. The enemy is textured differently. Criminal acts hide behind democratic functions. Lies posture as facts until proven otherwise. We can no longer use the word "comrade" without pondering upon it. Often, we have chosen not to use it.

The poets who appear in *Malibongwe* remind us of the cyclical nature of life. They urge us to ask ourselves; how many of the changes we have seen are the ones we really wanted? How many of the changes we welcomed have lost their significance? Just how much do we know about us, as people? How many of the changes we want sit like a mirage; too far to touch yet close enough to see?

Malibongwe may be a late returnee, but she is a welcome one. Hopefully libraries and archives in South Africa will bare their shelves in welcome as they stack her up in numbers. Thanks to Uhuru's vision, we can now sit with the book in our hands and revisit the past through poetry and work out for ourselves just how much of our past has continued into our present. And, when we work this out, we can hopefully do what poetry often does, and be pulled into action.

The work of compiling and editing *Malibongwe* deserves acknowledgement, study and accurate positioning with the current political and feminist literary conversations. This work pried open bolted doors. And these hands, I believe, deserve delicately perfumed, moisturising hand cream that we must offer in abundance. I also think that these hands can do with an energising massage. What would be best is to ask what these hands need and respond appropriately. For now, I offer my writerly gratitude to these hands. We know that the editor Sono/Lindiwe, in her poem "To a comrade", was as right back then as she is today:

> comrade
> there is no exit
> when the sounds of history
> curdle our blood

REFERENCES

Gilfillan, Lynda. "Black Women Poets in Exile: The Weapon of Words". *Tulsa Studies in Women's Literature*, 11, 1, 1992: 79–93.

Kgalane, Gloria Vangile. "Black South African Women's Poetry (1970–1991): A Critical Survey". Master's thesis, University of Johannesburg, 2012.

Mabuza, Lindiwe. *From ANC to Sweden*. Stockholm: Swedish Social Democratic Party, 1987

———— *Letter to Letta: Poems*.Johannesburg: Stokaville Publishers, 1991.

———— *Voices that Lead: 1976–1996*. Johannesburg: Vivlia, 1998.

———— *Africa to Me*. Wuppertal: Peter Hammer Verlag, 1998.

———— *Footprints and Fingerprints*. Northlands: Picador Africa, 2008

Musila, Grace A. "Chimamanda Adichie: The daughter of postcolonial theory." *Al Jazeera* online, 4 February 2018.

Ndebele, Njabulo S. *Rediscovery of the Ordinary Essays on South African Literature*. Scottsville: UKZN Press, 1991.

Nkondo, Sankie Dolly. *Flames of Fury and other Poems*. Fordsburg: Congress of South African Writers, 1990.

Xaba, Makhosazana. *Our Words, Our Worlds: Writing on Black South African Women Poets, 2000–2018*. Pietermaritzburg: UKZN Press, 2019.

FOREWORD *TO THE ORIGINAL EDITION*

SONO MOLEFE

SUDDENLY THERE ARE women poets from South Africa. Phenomenal, some might want to acclaim. Praise and accolades is not what these women are after. They clearly want your heart, eyes and nerves to move your mind to what they know, so that understanding afresh, you might be inclined to act accordingly. "We are exploited and oppressed", is what the collective voice states on behalf of those whose cries and words are muffled by bullet sounds plus fascist manoeuvres to bluff the unwitting. "We shall be free" is the tough fibre that binds those on both sides of the Apartheid divide.

But who are these women? As any of them will tell, they are no striking personalities individually. Yet as part of the face of the liberation movement of South Africa, the African National Congress (ANC-SA), they are simply formidable. They come to the world then, in the main, as members of the ANC. The names are there but that is only a partial story since full identity will only be possible after South Africa is free, and with genuine democracy.

For the moment suffice it to say there are those who battled police, their dogs and bullets on the streets of their country in 1976. There are students and former school-teachers. There are trained soldiers, daughters of workers, militant patriots fully engaged in the continuous act of liberation, one and all, struggle is their chosen path. The age range also represents that steady mounting dynamism of the oppressed of that land: a fifteen year old as assured of direction, unwavering side by side with a fifty year old, all challenging hurdles with energy derived from a tested and winning ideological perspective, affirming, questioning, developing ideas, forging ahead towards a victory no power on earth can deny the people of South Africa.

There is no romance here, though all attest a love deeply rooted in their usurped land. No academic optimism where illusory easy victories are spun out of pseudo-revolutionary theories! No unwarranted pessimism in the context of international and continental struggles. Only pounding reality, now unpalatable – now lifting, but always moving towards the known to-be-known ultimate success of the African Revolution. These lovers, then, speak as one. But since this collective voice also means people, we hope you can hear and know the distinct voice through each individual emphasis, pitch, tone, syntax and idiom for these are singular voices too. Find them. Discover some peculiarities. Then love the harmony of song. Because in many exciting ways, these specific weights of melody blend into a ponderable sweetness of heavy harmony, rich symphony – a style and aesthetic that are thrillingly new: nerve-filled and public.

What we have then is a poetry bound up intimately with all their people's lives. We have a people impelled by the greatest vision there is: the total liberation of men, women and children – a country.

The poems also want to enter the nerve of the defenders and apologists of Apartheid, split it asunder with the panorama of extensive, conscious genocidal practices of the regime. Without South Africa's present political aberrations of justice and equality none of the voices in this collection would have opted for exile.

Yet because exile is transitory it is almost embraceable. But embraceable only as necessities that school, meetings that prepare one for the arduous task ahead. Exile and alienation are seen in relation to the fundamental alienation of the overwhelming working majority in South Africa from land, cultural wealth, wholesomeness – wholeness; all the products of that majority's sweat and blood – through general deprivation and exclusion from decisions affecting the people's lives. In this sense there is no self-pity. It is this political awareness and engagement with all aspects of South Africa that rescues their perspective from self-devouring individualism and from whining weakness.

This also accounts to some extent for the general tone of the collection which remains solidly communal. The public voice starts with people, revolves around them, peers into our eyes to see whether or not we refuse to see the ghastly deeds of "civilisation". Obviously these authors have a mission. Critical of the status quo, offering solutions, they offer no apologies for being supporters of the destruction of exploitation of man by man in their country, undivided.

If at the same time there is no conformity to "accepted" poetry norms in their message it is because mainly those acquainted with elements of traditional poetics would fully appreciate the mode within which some poems are written. The rhetorical style of a number of the poems is a case in point. Because of the oral and hence public nature of traditional poetry, it has its own poetics, quite different from that conducive to quiet reading in one's study. Yet it is not a contradiction to say that even when read individually or privately, the poems still have spark to fire one in one's study, and the energy to move one from the study and merely studying. The art of these poems is, in part, their verbal structures that are shaped to be skilful oral agents as well as reminders. They are re-creative.

Many of the poems have been heard inside South Africa over Radio Freedom, the broadcast services of the African National Congress operating through the generosity and solidarity of several African states. In military training camps, the value of some has been firmly attested to by the applause from the exclusively South African audiences there. A few were heard at the Eleventh International Festival of Youth and Students in Cuba. Such poetry has always raised moral, giving impetus and emotional stimuli and dimensions to political content. Through this cultural medium, political consciousness has been elevated in many. So be it, women.

Amandla!

1982

AFRICA SHALL BE FREE

Masechaba
Ilva Mackay

Africa
mother of children
impatient
reluctant
to be like the rivers that
meander to the seas

Africa
mother of children
destitute
dying but
determined
to prescribe themselves freedom
to describe themselves free

Africa
your children no longer nestle in your arms
crawl on your belly
accept their fate (dumb, silent)
your children have rejected their garments
of indifference
of docile acceptance
your children no longer (your children) sleep and do not sleep

Africa
the voice of your children
erodes the mist-shrouded mountains
like hungry rain
and cuts through the valleys
like the pounding rivers
that ravage and rape your fields

Africa
today your rivers heal our wounds
your fields offer us refuge
and your mountains do not silence, no they hold and harbour
the sounds of warriors answering the call for justice.

Mangaung
Lindiwe Mabuza

I was born on January the 8th
For my birth
My parents traveled
Days and long miles
To a place called
Mangaung
Which means
The meeting place of the leopards

Today,
The enemy calls my cradle
Bloemfontein.
Mangaung was warm
Hospitable
A meeting place
Where now
Only poisonous crops
Of injustice
Bloom

Well,
Just for me
One January 8th
My parents came
From all corners heights and plains
Of our land
Stolen
And in pain...

Our cattle gone
Our homes burnt
Our fields made green by us
But especially not for us
And if they could only speak,
All those rivers of South Africa
Could tell of countless seasons
Of our blood, our tears

But that's when my parents
Were not married.
They walked alone,
Just like each fighting bulldozer alone
Alone, tried to brave
With bare hands
The mad stampede of elephants
When single-handed victories
Often leave each parent armless
If alive at all...

But before that January 8th
After the enemy
Settled a little family quarrel he had
Over our EVERYTHING
He united
And strengthened his fighting muscle
Against my people

Today
English French Dutch
German Italian Greek
Portuguese and other
Tongues of Europe
Pronounce themselves
Nation – indivisible
In my country!
And us –
Sotho Venda Xhosa Pedi
Tsopi Shangaan Zulu
The same European tongues
Pronounce
Nations – divisible
In my country!

Oh,
But just for my birth
Serious anxious and colourful parents
Were there,
They came
On foot on bicycle
Oxwagons horseback
Some by trains with cattle, like cattle,
Through rains and the frying sun...
The wind thorns and rock
Sand too they conquered,
They came
The flame-hearted ones,
The back-bent and bruised ones
Their unseen scars swelling anew

The whipped ones came
The down-trodden
Violated again and again
Though unyielding
Whenever tried like reeds
In the cruel whirls and storms
Of Anglo-Boer love
They arrived,
These unconquerable custodians of justice
And rallied
Their vision fixed on a gigantic
A pregnant idea!

Down from the place
Of another birth
The birth of dispossession
Called Natal
They came with stories
Of how the valley of a thousand hills
Always green and swollen with hope
Seemed to swallow Tugela waters
Just to let freedom riders pass!
And those whose wagons and bicycles
Saw the Lekwa and Nciba waters
Rise
With African pride
Also impatient for return of stolen banks
Whispered in various tongues
That even creatures
Known to love human blood
Popped their heads high

Up and down
Spirited by the call of
MANGAUNG
And bubbled
Deep in their water-home
Ndlelanhla!
Just to let the freedom riders pass!
Titlela a ti basi
Tsela Tsweu
Just to let the freedom riders pass!
Just to lighten the burden
Ndila tsena
Let the roads be white
They all sang
Just to let the freedom riders pass.

They came
Burning deep inside
In the hidden brow
Watery in the hidden eye
Weighted on the mind
By what they called
The pains of labour

From pass-carrying mines
From pass-carrying farms
From pass churches, pass schools
pass university, pass stores, pass laws
From plenty heavy pass work
Our people did and still do,
Speaking all the despised languages

Of our roots
And European ones too
They arrived

All their hearts pounding
All thoughts now extended, mingling
All embracing now
Awaiting
The beginning of the death of our
Splitting pain
The pain that separates us
Awaiting,
The birth of our nation
There at MANGAUNG!

I think my parents
Chose this place because
I was to be special
The first fruit of peace
From ourselves to ourselves
The living wedding gift
An unbreakable vow
That each is empowered
And raised higher
Only
And then only
In the tightening and linking
Of our clenched fists:
In short
A weapon against
Divide and destroy

Today,
The enemy greases the pockets
Of a few greedy ones
Who wear our leopard skins
And forget MANGAUNG!
The enemy dots our country
With smallpox and leprosy
Dumps
Called Bantustans
To hasten the death
Of our nation!

But I'm an extraordinary spirit
A power, a force, a home
A shield
A spear
A child
Yes, a child born with stubborn leopard spots
Of racism
All over
But born nonetheless
Breathing, kicking, stretching

Into the future
Breathing heavily
With the hearts of leopards and lions
Plus all the known
And unknown courage and triumphs
Of Africa
For I was born
At the gathering of the brave!

Today,
The enemy tramples
On the burial place
Of our umbilical cord
With iron boots tanks
And bullet-belts

Oh no!
Please!
I'm not boasting
When I say
I have the most supreme family tree
For every vein in my body
Every artery was infused with blood
Rich
With the history of freedom fighters.
And just for my birth
They all came!
Thulimahasha was there
Remembering Soshangane
Sikhukhuni stood high
Our kinds standing taller
And more majestic
Than any Hollywood king of kings
Makhado with his elephants head
He remembered Thohoyandou
Khama, Moshoeshoe
All shielding the lowly victims of
Capital and race
Victims of bloodsucking exploitation
Cetshwayo with unshakeable Shaka

On his mind
All took off
Their cloak of loneliness
Hintsa, Makhanda Nxele
Their leopard flesh touching close
And all carrying
The spear of the nation

And then
To think
All of them
All in me
This wealth, this vast greatness
Our country, our people
All in each of us,
Whatever our birth
Wherever our birth
Whenever we struggle wherever we carry the struggle
For I was born
Crying FREEDOM!
While our working people
The true midwives of our wealth
Midwives of vision, hope
Our future
Tenderly passed me
From hand to joining hand
Of leopard hearts
Blowing into me
The rising strains of
Nkosi Sikelel' iAfrika

And
What's my name?

The AFRICAN NATIONAL CONGRESS
of South Africa. Born January
8, 1912.
I gave birth to UMKHONTO
WE SIZWE on the 16th of December
1961.

Umkhonto
Baleka Kgositsile

Rhythm
sound
from the drums in our distant past
still air
threatened by colonial vultures
rhythm
I inherited and now
I give in this umbilical cord
this dance has been with us
long before our ancestors
saw the day
rhythm
this dance will be with us
long after we are silent
and our memories
remain like day or night
in the heart of the future

Rhythm
feet so precise
to the left
to the right
to the songs
we sing now
our voices beckoned
from the past of the future
will be pronounced
medicine or poison

rhythm
this dance is our future
moving with the clumsy
or graceful vigour of the present
to the song of today
echoed in our tomorrow
rhythm
we are all artists
on this stage
there is no break
to this dance

What is that sound that appeals
the peals of thunder
in my stomach
my child's motive anxiety to live
this rhythm
whose brutality
anger
and resolve
flow in my veins
through this umbilical cord
rhythm
to the sound of those heavy drops
from millions of black bodies
to the tears of emaciated children
to the endless sweat of the toiling parents
to the blood of the heroes

in this dance
rhythm

Yes
our today's dance
towards a better tomorrow
is dictated by yesterday
rhythm
what was that note
still fresh in
the morning air of Africa
the beginning of the end
of the stench of colonialism
rhythm
only yesterday my brothers
from Angola to Mozambique
danced a protracted step
to the song
of exploitation

What is this song
colliding in the air
with the worker's song
of a better tomorrow
rhythm
to the futile obstinacy
of the imperialism
of the flight
of the neo-colonial ghost
when the dance of the present
has carried us safely

to the people's tomorrow
rhythm
is the unison
in the step
and the harmony
in the song
from all depths and corners
of capitalist plunder
RESISTANCE

Rhythm that gave birth to us
and the dance we bear
we make this choice and no apology
love to this song
song of the bazooka
that carries familiar notes with
rhythm
of consistency
since 1652
to the pregnancy of the people's
dignity and sanity
and the birth of
"one that responds when called"

What is the law of the present
we sing and swim in this redness
that has brought us here
we dive and duck
this is our dance to the
rhythm
of centuries of NO!

to oppression
this is the dance of now
in the bush
in the city
in the ghetto
in the kitchen
in the factory
this is today's dance to the
rhythm
that gave birth to the
peasants and workers
that lead the dance to the
song of impatience
to NO! now in the voice of thunder
as the people's anger
pumps out gallons of pus
from the traitor's body

Rhythm
spat out by the gun
that sings liberation for the people
in the hands of my father
who danced in Wankie to the
rhythm
of the birth of MK
that has the grenades and guns
that sing the song
my people want to hear
in the hands of my sister
who danced to the fascist bullet
that silenced Hector Peterson

to the ranks of the exiled and MK
and the song of hope
in the hands of
ZAPU, ZANU, SWAPO, PLO, POLISARIO

After this dance
the sound of our satisfaction
in clearer mornings
of future generations
centuries of applause
as the songs of jubilation
bury this rot
songs of our clean bones
scattered all over our land giving
rhythm
and direction to the dance of then
it is now's motive song in us
our right to
DIE TODAY TO LIVE TOMORROW

December Sixteen
Lindiwe Mabuza

Comrades
I was not there
On December 16, 1961
And you probably were not there either

We neither heard Mandela's trumpet
Stirring and mustering to national duty
Millions of poised waiting lions
Nor were we in Tambo's mind
As he carried us around the globe
Dissecting for the world to see
Our land and fields overflowing
With rivers and rivers
Of our own precious blood.
Perhaps, we didn't even feel
The pounding hammering thrill
Inside Sisulu's heart
As he helped forge
And *wield* UMKHONTO WE SIZWE

But comrades
Though we were not there
At those meandering underground journeys
Voyages into the daylight of victory
No comrades
Absent, we were very much there
For we recall now and relive today
The supreme challenge

Of the true leader of our people
Chief Albert Mvumbi Luthuli
When that magnificent giant of a lion roared
And the thunder and tremor of his words
Still echo in our consciences, our consciousness
This day
"I am an African
And if the enemy comes into my home
To attack both myself and my family
Then I as an African
Must take up my spear and fight"

Yes comrades
Absent we were there
Because we all now agree
That this pain
Will not repair
Before the sharpening of our spears
Deep inside racist and fascist bones
To hunt and haunt the enemy
Out of our home, our social equal home.

A new child is born
Gloria Mtungwa

Pushing and kicking
violently...
causing sometimes
       pain
at times
       joy
sometimes
       curses

The sweet-sorrow
of childbirth
bearing a bundle of happiness
love and prosperity

The indescribable
feeling
in moments
of anguish
wishing it was over
and done with

A few months
that seem
a few weeks
fewer days
nearer to
liberty from
bearing a baby
long overdue

One pitiful scream
a push
and the child
is born
the future
OUR SHIELD
OUR SPEAR
OUR MK

Born out of sorrow
the liberator
the victor
over squalor, grief and subjection
the harbinger
of
love, sunshine and equality.
MK
our MK.

BIRTH AND GENOCIDE

For my unborn child
Baleka Kgositsile

Mound of life
    rise like the tide of revolution
Mound of life
    come join us
    as sure as the day of liberation

Lands far from your forefathers'
embrace you and feed you
as they will
it is not your fault
but it will be a crime
if in your lifetime
you do not fight
back to the land of your forefathers

My screams go up
    the labour of my people
The pain
    the struggle
    the blood
The cry of determination
    from the bottom of the pile
    the women of our land
Life on the beautiful land

"There is no birth without blood"
There is no blood without pain
    I add
When the streets and rivers of our land turn red
    it will be the dawn of the day
Our land will kiss freedom welcome

I labour with all the mothers
    whose children's cherished lives
Were ended with the callous ease
    known only by a fascist
To them I bear hundreds of sons
    who will be Africa's sun

To the fascist I scream
    the labour of my people
The pain
    the struggle
    the blood
The scream of my people's determination
    splits fascist eardrums

Exhausted by the battle of labour
   with untold satisfaction
      I kiss you welcome
With dreams and hopes
   born with each determined kick and move
      with each ripple on my stomach
         like the anger of my people
Mound of life
   come join us
Together we must hunt the fascist down
   cut his deaf head off
      and let life flow in our land

Black, eleven, and sterile
Lindiwe Mabuza

because your colour is your jew
i dare not think too long of you

legs of ash
long, like winter's willows thinned –
thighs of black pools, want pooled
unknowing, thighs stained again and again
by banquets and banquets
of sickle cells of unjustice
what shall i say
when you're grown
what shall i say
when you ask
"why mama, why?
did i menopause when you signed
that slip at the doctor's for the
office of equal opportunity?"

tadpole bodies flowing, like reaching cedars pleasing
flowing reaching pleasing
hopping and bruising but always rising,
we saw you skip
like some unbridled thoughts
we leapt with you on time
beyond the frenzied air of Nixon's grip
babygirl babysister womanchild
because your colour leaps
round and around like the yeast of jazz we swung

past the feast of satiated sharks
behind a diseased slave ship
this way and that way but always rising,
rising with battalions
from the heat-beaten stretches of Alabama
daring dare with millions
in the south of Africa
where little girls are unmothered at birth
womanchild
because your colour is your jew
they will excavate the mines of our being
babygirl
because your colour is your jew
because Hitler is a neon-bladed hydra
dare we enter your field,
warm,
dare we climax without tears,
consummated,
dare we think long of the shapes and shades of pumpkin
waiting in the flower
impatient for the wind and sun and water –
in the spring of your truant yearnings
waiting?

i dare not think too long of you
because your colour is your jew

not a word! not a word!
and he never said a mumbling word!
here was the tender skin
just below the navel...

first the white doctor's eyes measured

then a surgical hand slashed

separating flesh from flesh

squirting blood from the reservoir of fresh warriors...

the pomegranate chambers bleed the blood of green –

never again! not a word!

the little woman cannot feel herself recoil

as the doctor pulls and pulls and pulls;

up, up, up... there...

dragging us down into

drunk ovens

leaping ovens

unchosen land

land-of-the-chosen land

choice uterus land

sizzling land that broils brains and wombs

land where children know death's labour

before the lessons of the moon

there...

the hand that knows

the hand that writes

unleashes the best ties...

and overhead knot here

a blackwall hitch here

perhaps a loop there (for the boy scouts of the USA)

to anchor our blooming lobes

into an eternal limbo!

there!

now each sperm must slowly knock

then die in our empty womb.

our virgin lands were ravaged and raped
the seed will not stir to dance!
womb of my race
target of their hate
womb of my race

forever they scrub you clean...
clean womb, clean teeth, clean USA-South Africa
and little black girls have paid the price
for the whitening of America.
and we here have paid taxes
for the pruning of the poor!

i dared not, not think of you
because your colour is my jew

oh! the bitter screams of strangled truths
they hurt to the very womb!
oh! the daily drowning and draining
it calls for a major operation!
this foundation, time-eaten and festering
must face millions of fishers of justice –
it calls for a major operation!
this roof here can no longer protect
from men or beast or wind or rain
oh! the daily drowning and draining
"the whole Jericho road must change!"

we dare not think of you
because the semite is our colour

yes! thoughts may dull the pain
but what we need are those that suck
the dams of pain...
what we need are pyramids of hands to wrench
the belly of oppression...
what we need is you, and you, and you too to RAM a resounding   NO!
to ALL in the world
who murder through laws!   NO!
who starve through laws!   NO!
who dispossess through laws!   NO!
who miseducate through laws!   NO!
who kill by giving drugs to children!   NO!
who institutionalise VD at TUSKEGEE for black guinea pigs!   NO!
who hate the poor for getting poorer!   NO!
who love the rich for getting richer!   NO!

what we need is you, and you, and you too
to work for a world that is a fertile womb
    yet always always pregnant for the best yes...

NOTES:
- In 1973, revelations were made about the non-consensual sterilisations of two black sisters in Alabama, USA, aged eleven and twelve. The doctor performing the operation was employed by the Office of Equal Opportunity (OEO) of the USA federal government
- Over a 25-year period in Tuskegee, Mississippi, USA, white doctors secretly carried out experiments on black patients presenting with venereal disease (VD). They divided them into "control" and "experiment" groups, allowing VD to take its own course with the "experiment" group, while treating the "control" group.

Tribal customs
Phyllis Altman

She was fourteen
When they tore the ovaries
From her living body

Then sent her to a brothel
For the use of Nazi soldiers

She was twenty
When I saw her
She did not speak

Each day
She washed dressed fed
cleaned

Placed in a chair in the garden
When the weather was fine

When I approached she smiled

A smile so apprehensive
So appeasing

A smile of such total terror

That if you had seen it
You would not dare
To presume yourself
Superior

One life lost
Jumaimah Motaung

Three o'clock
The darkest hour
The crow of a cock
The cry of a baby
Hungry sick
Also the mother

The dawn of a dark day
Misery's spouse
The crying baby's body
Hang on the light scales
of Kwashiokor
Who knows? Who knows?
From the corner of the day the cockerel crows

The mother awakes
Confused film in her eyes
Drives her to join her baby's
Cries
She folds his tears
Under her hands
Death in her head
Walks over the land

SPIRIT OF SOWETO:
THE GHETTO, MASSACRES; RESOLVE

I must go: do not mourn
Fezeka Makonese

Weep no more
Mama dear weep no more
How importune the lightning
The stroke of the hour of parting
My age urges me
I will go
So please mother dear
Weep no more

Weep not mother
It is the clarion call
The distant light
Is bearing my name
Towards our goal
It is for your comfort too
That I go now
Already gone are my contemporaries
Some never to rise again

Schoolmates have fallen! All fallen?
There in the steps of our forebears!
These roses and other flowers
In your garden urge me to go
They evoke memories of wreaths:
So do not enchain me with tears;
Other youths keep calling my name
Please let me go ma
Mother dear weep no more

At this point Mama dear
Having seen terror and raging horror
In all my few living days
I know that the rifle
Has got to be carried
Across many backs:
How will I live long days
If it by-passes me
Many seeking the light
Have fallen before their dawn
And I must go

That the unborn child
May not see what I see
Or taste what I've tasted
This is my journey

Stay well, ma!

Soweto road
Lindiwe Mabuza

On this spot rough
from cares of slow years
on these streets
muddy from torrents red
on these crooked roads
yawning for direction
here where like early spring
awaiting rain's seeds
young voices stormed horizons
how yet like summer streams
young blood flowed over
flooded flower
in the dead of winter

On this road here
here this road here
tingles and shudders
from acid taste
the snakeskin snakestooth whiplash road where snakes tongue flicker lick
broken glass children's park
road school for shoeless feet...
olympic track perfected
by daily daring sprints
against passes
and barbed wire nakedness...
this road pressed soft
oozing like tear-falls
treeless showground for hardware processions
all the June sixteen festivals

and their mad array of hippos
muffling contrary anthems
with machine-gun chatter
naked greed and lust for blood in camouflage
Soweto road drunk
from rich red wine
this sweet arterial blood
for choice Aryan folk...
battlefield road here yes

Here
yes even here
where road-blocks to life pile
precariously
here we kneel
scoop earth raise mounds of hope
we oath
with our lives
we shall immortalise
each footprint left each grain of soil that flesh shed here
each little globe of blood
dropped in our struggle
upon the zigzag path of revolution...
Soweto blood red road
will not dry up
until the fields of revolution
fully mellow tilled
always to bloom again

Fallen hero
Gloria Nkadimeng

you have fallen warring comrade
breaking life's string between you and me
you who lay down one beloved life
for twenty million lives this motherland
you comrade justice and courage

i'll not blot this motherland with a tear
over you... nor now
but will mobilise my will

you were silenced because of your truthful tongue
you who tore down unmasked the wall-paper-white-wash sense
of slave education
and what of the silver-coated frame of tribalism you abhorred
what of it?
you spared neither effort nor life
to crush the architects these barbarous wizards
now here you life lifeless in a fertile grave
of twenty million hearts
    now i'll not burden you with the ticking minutes
    of teargas in our youthful eyes
    the whizzing brutality of bullets that was the day
no i'll not
i'll be silent like the silenced that (now) you are
but i'll ricochet in fury
boomerang to bury this death once and for all!

Childhood in Soweto
Lerato Kumalo

There are no playgrounds
no parks
but plenty dust
children compete
cars bicycles hungry mongrels
narrow streets and garbage
there is no childhood
in Soweto

There are no stars
to twinkle twinkle little eyes
no rockets
launch dreams
no new year resolutions rise
through the thick
blanket of smoke
in Soweto
dust aplenty

There is no poverty
of sirens
sprinters' footsteps
coattail-ends whisk away
jack-boot doors howl
men women children terrorised
huddled in raids
bundled in rage
passes passes passes

there is no childhood
no adulthood
in Soweto
only plenty
dust

But I have seen new plays
in one act
announcing the birth
of childhood
grenades clearing the night
of blinders of smoke
and hurdles
passing the child
into star-grappling teens
adulthood without passes
in Soweto
in towns and cities
north and east
growing from
Soweto

Soweto wishes
Lindiwe Mabuza

Please put a gun
In this itching hand
For I almost tasted victory
When the enemy dazed...
But wordspears and stones
Cannot pierce
The heart of our pain

Somebody please place weapons
In these palms that just toyed with rattles
While lullabies were hummed
For I too have heard songs
Rise from Angolan wars won
But their refrain
Will not drown
Some echoes from the homefront battlefield

With gun in hand
I could feel the fire of joy
For I would be one with many
Whose tears I must drain
Those tearing screams
From disemboweled bodies
Must be hushed forever

Please let me bear its weight
On my growing shoulders
For although I'm only a cub

I have worn the armour of man
Knowing the deeds of years
That were planted
Have fertilised our land

With new dawn's energy
I must strengthen my sinews
For I have seen creatures stampede
And build icebergs in Liberty's path
But volcanic tides will charge
Making love to our own ploughs
Which must furrow for life

Venceremos
Ilva Mackay

Had you seen our children
mowed by bullets
gassed and beaten
armed with stones
and dust-bin lids
where lead took lives
but did not end in death
you will know why we fight

If you see the prisons
where night-time voices
echo across the quadrangles
strength emanating from their sons
where we are one
in our determination to be free,
you will know
why we continue undeterred

If you see our mothers
the widows and
the fighters
soldiering on day by day
giving life to the Mashambas
                    and Mahlangus
you will know
that we shall win

Mother Patriot (June 16th, 1976, Soweto)
Rebecca Matlou

I saw yesterday
with sockets wet protruding
from a hollow shack a woman spread
into wilderness fists
teeth
to face death.
Skies hurled fires of doom
mountain mounds of poison
quaked shuddered
me you us
cloven-clumped to hang roots
hunched beards crawled away
toddlers
crept strode
nearer the form
to bring their budding
tomorrow now

What is this today, what was yesterday
shall tomorrow dawn to set for them?
Who ever prophesied this black cloud
this stiletto tear all of her here apart
how could mother-wife patriot human being woman
cow to the blanket of oblivion

how could...

Death drops scarlet
on the barren earth
engraved onto younglings' palm words

"She must be avenged."

Years of the child
Baleka Kgositsile

South Africa
let our children live
let the young bones in
Dimbaza scream
let the blood of '76
drown the killers
let the young imprisoned
or exiled drink your milk
the bitter milk of yesterday
to make them grow
like a veldfire
let it flow in every
young vein and artery
that they be firm in
name and nationality
let them drink the milk
known by the warriors of Isandlwana
Mother
Home
your children
of whom your richness
stripped you
let your anxious breast
knead you together
let them itch
with the salt of
your sweat and tears

let our future burn in them
that they create
years of the child
let their hunger
bear their anger
let our children live
and live

Mayibuye
Ilva Mackay

Mayibuye...
the sons and daughters of Africa remained hopeful
one day
some day
our mother will be returned to us

Yesterday
armed with stones
    and determination
the voices of freedom
echoed from
Soweto to Cape Flats
Gelvandale to KwaMashu
as Vorster's henchmen
murdered man and child

Today
the sons and daughters of Africa
embrace the weapons of our struggle
with guns and truth
and swear
that our mother shall be returned to us

WOMEN IN STRUGGLE

Women arise
Alice Tsongo

Women of our land arose
heard call of distant drums
summoning to unity
to war oppressive laws

1913 call
vibrated from eardrum to ear
they arose those warrior-women
and marched into the "Free State"...
eyes blazing they hammered forward
their path, and racists quivered.
The women blazed nearer and
nearer
forcing the final cowards
to burn that violent law
their special restrictive permits of paper
that arrested human movement.

Forty years later
we were there
holding the fort... fiercely again, women
Lilian and Helen
who followed Charlotte Maxeke
leading our women to apex: August fifty-six

Women arose
thoughts bathed in sweat they marched
twos and threes of colours
coming, coming

torrents of defiance
to the very contaminated steps of Pretoria's Union Buildings
they marched

Petitions submitted
Strydom re-whitened
looked, then preferred to hide...
taught his secretary lies... "Out on business!"

Bravery kept vigil
night transforming to triumph
how did their beings know
police dogs were watching, waiting
for the slightest move to jump
against that victory!
Mothers can march to battle!
WOMEN OF AFRICA, ARISE!

NOTES:

- "Lilian" refers to Lilian Ngoyi. Born in 1911 to a mine worker, she was a leading member of the Garment Workers' Union, one of the key volunteers during the ANC-lead Defiance Campaign Against Unjust Laws of 1952. By the time of her untimely death, 12 March,1980, Lilian was the President of the Federation of South African Women and President of the African National Congress Women's League. In 1954, she was the prime mover, leading 20 000 women of all races to confront the Prime Minister Strydom in protest against passes. Known and most beloved internationally, tributes flowed in from all parts of the world, paying respect to the great heroine of our struggle, Lilian Masediba Ngoyi.
- "Helen" refers to Helen Joseph. Still dangerous to the regime when she turned 75 on 8 April 1980, she remained a source of inspiration to freedom fighters. She was the first person ever to be placed under house arrest by the fascist regime, and was banned and jailed innumerable times.
- Charlotte Maxeke was a founding member of the African National Congress on 8 January 1912 at Mangaung (Bloemfontein), and the first woman member of the ANC National Executive Committee. She was the main organiser and leader of the 1913 Anti-Pass Campaign.

Militant beauty
Gloria Mtungwa

Fragility, flimsy womanhood
flowers on her birthdays
luxurious apartments and flashy cars
have never been her aspiration

Distorted women's lib
refusing to mother kids
and provide family comfort
harassing a tired enslaved dad
have never been her deeds.

Attending to the needs
however meagre they might be
slaving for their well-being
pretending abuses don't mean a thing
her only aspiration
keeping candle light burning

Hardened by oppressive regime
she refuses to weep
even at death of innocents
who continue age-old fight for justice
her only aspiration... liberty.

Standing defiantly
in face of brutality
resulting from corrupt illegal minority.

Flowering in natural beauty
through progressive ideology
she overcame imposed passivity
and became the essence of militancy

Her beauty is not her criterion
but justice for all humanity, person to person.

Super-women (Grown by apartheid)
Lindiwe Mabuza

she
    wakes up each morning
    to the vacant sound of the beetle
    always teasing with the false alarm
    the dry ashes which
    conceal in their fine frailty
    the live calender
    of mealless meals
    do you recall stranger

a traveler's stomach is the size of a gizzard?

she
    often washes her face
    with touches of saliva
    before licking the sleep-glued sight of her baby...
    do you recall stranger
    the roar in the veins of pain?

she
    moves, stranger in her country
    empty...
    even calabashes follow her shrinking gaze open-
    mouthed
    everyday everywhere
    beleaguered by laws and
    bound to infant and hut
    she must face a land criss-crossed
    and dissected by droughts

even here on these expanses
where ancestors once feasted
plotted
and fought

vainly
rerouting
the erosions coming
to these super-women
of our super-exploited regions...
listen to their song stranger...

without a man
i am man
without a husband
i am husband-wife
without a father
children might grow
without other hands
the earth must bring forth
without without without always
i must be without

she
husbands the frigid lands
while her body sucks in
summer's fury
beneath the scorched soles of her furrowed
feet

the mirage speeds up its snake dance
 even as the sun seems to stomp
 hypnotically
 upon the crown of her head
 dazing her thoughts
 also hungry

she
 erects the pick
 beyond the listless fly-eyes bundle
 on her back about the age of dr. death's
 visitation... always on call
 on these lands

she
 lowers her sharp thirsty hope on obstinate grounds
 where it rebounds
 also her pick
 like all her other pleas
 leaving a solo tone to the tune hollow
of these super-women
of our super-exploited land...
do you hear her song?
 without without without always
 i must be without

do you think she gets angry at
 the earth sometimes
  and its surfaces?
sprawling
 softened by tears and also
 salivation for human flesh

the land produces steady harvests of
    graves
     asking
doomed or not doomed?

we have seen her
    lashing at her birth
    when faster than vultures can descend on yesterday
    death triumphs over today's scraggy steers
death by hunger and thirst
    where ivory tower righteousness hangs
over the super-women
    of our super-exploited land
    groaning under an iron yoke
    without without without always
    they must be without

we abide on the perimeters of paradise
    but cannot wear the free robes of rights
    of our hands
    though we sweat diamonds into crowns
    of these human gods
    who would award us with death wishes
till somehow
    often, our lives add up to dry
    webs
keeping guard over
    haunting memories
those that sometimes arrive
    "special delivery" in a casket
    as when dust has exploded inside miners'
    lungs

they have no computers
    for tears
    in the dumping grounds
of South Africa
where children scramble for
    garbage
only records of
    "superfluous appendages"
and desexed marriage
    hostels
    that breed apartheid studs

There are no libraries for
    gold mine legends
but our lives are
    shelved repositories
    of imfirmities
    of pass books
    which sum the reserves
    value
    of "temporary sojourners"
    working to be deported to die away from the country
    we
    chiselled while it billows-in
    angry napalm on
    future features
of these super-women
of our super-exploited land where over and again
the roar of hunger silences

    without without without always
    they must be without

there is mounting anger
    on paths that frame desolation:
    strong and stern the faces unshroud
    revealing a blaze concealed by custom
    and time

she, the woman
    marches from many paths
    untying knots
    sickling tied overgrowths of want

she, the woman, the man
    exorcises the land
    possessed by the madmen of history
    the classes convulse
    the mine marriages dissolve
    and the exonerated reef
    fling
    to the mountain tops
    the burnished sons of the land
    with her together
    they claim our land
    they reclaim the wastelands
    with bold boulders of
    righteousness
    and glory-to-man-woman

with her, the woman
    they scoop the earth into their hands
    they mold it
    they coddle it
    they stop to marvel at its exhilarated soft
    suns and sums

until in their own hands
    the land moves
    from hand to hand
    the land moves
    from child to child
    the land grows
    from woman to man
    from man to woman
    it explodes into beaded bubbles
    of peace
    and from that sprouts of
    gigantic palms
    broadcast
    their peaceful arms equally
    banishing alms

with her, the woman
    the sea of people bend
    (also the straight and narrow path of trials)
    placing their marvel
    and handiwork
    over the grave of exploitation
    guarded by the tombstone of superwoman

with her forever
    they sing the amen of vigilance

with all
　　i am
　　with man
　　i am human
　　with husband
　　i am wife
with father
　　the children must grow
　　with other hands
　　the earth brings forth
　　without without
　　we will no longer be
　　without

NOTES:

- The notion of the rural African woman as superwoman derives from the fact that, while she has to perform all the tasks traditionally relegated to women, she also has to be much more. Since all the able-bodied males are recruited as part of contract labour, rural African women in particular must also perform men's work, just as their male counterparts may have to perform traditional women's work in the urban areas.

The great day (August 9th)
Jumaimah Motaung

Your Mother, my Mother
Our mothers,
Marching...
They heard the call
They came together and shared ideas
They all had one aim in mind
To show the regime
They were not what the regime thought they were – robots.

One husband might have reprimanded the wife,
"What do you people think you are up to?"
And the wife might have answered bravely,
"We know our aims and objectives
We mean to carry them out"
Your Mother and my Mother.

The day dawned,
Staunch...
They marched,
"To the Union Buildings"
They had heard the commanding tone
And indeed they went
Carrying us on their backs
Gallant heroes of the time
Courageous they were
Women from all walks of life.
Your Mother, My Mother
Our Mothers.

To our Mothers!
Mpho Maruping

Weep not mothers,
Painful, yes it is,
What Vorster and Smith
Are doing to you
Harassing and slaughtering
Mothers, be brave!
Tread on the steps of
Lilian Ngoyi, Dorothy Nyembe,
Helen Joseph and Paulina Mogale.

What has befallen you
Might befall me,
Let us not relax.
Our country must be liberated
Like Angola and Mozambique.
Mothers!
South Africa Zimbabwe Namibia
Are waiting for us
To take up arms.

Vorster has toughened you
He has taught you miseries,
You will learn to carry an RPG-7,
You will use it to lull a baby,
That baby will be a new South Africa.

Ode to Aunt Mary
Anonymous

For seventeen years
she had to live in isolation
among her community

For seventeen years
she had to stay in the prison
that was the Transvaal

For seventeen years
she had to wear the heavy shawl
of a banned person

A banned woman
A banned wife
A banned black-mother

Up to her dying day
shown no mercy
up to her dying day

And some claim
this is a Christian country
and others claim
this is a Christian government

But we know it is not
and so does Aunt Mary Moodley
and all those restricted
and listed persons
hundreds and more
who wear the claw-marks
scratched crimson on their lives
by a "Christian law"!

NOTES:

- On 23 October 1979, Aunt Mary Moodley passed away, leaving a rich history of struggle emanating from her deep warmth and love for people and an even deeper hatred of the system that wrecked, then discarded humans. Multiple arrests and banning orders did not stop her grassroots organising.

Dedication
Susan Lamu

Mother of freedom Helen
At seventy-three still a threat
What savagery aimed against her
Bullets, batons, shattering windows

Helen Joseph has defeated aggression,
Her soul is free from racial contamination,
Mother, lover of freedom
Dauntless ever,
Look at her refusing bread in old age
Eating rock
With the downtrodden,
Her heart grows fonder, profounder

Her face is carved from steel
Her eye is gentle and brave
She enters the dock, stands still
Listens carefully: the indictment read...
It says nothing, nothing base about her
Not anything to brand her foe of the people,
The people she lovingly serves.
So she swallows and takes a deep breath.

We are winning the battle!
Down to the dark cell she strides
The Amandla trumpet behind her
Blowing, blowing, blowing...

Fighting woman
Duduzile Ndelu

Brilliant daughter of Africa
Fighting woman of our land
Hunted across the country
Once
By ever frenzied Special Branch hiding behind laws
Who now have their pound of flesh behind bars
Their pound of flesh on scales of blood behind walls of writing
But still Dorothy, age-old African victim and victor
You still instill fear in their hearts.

Fearless sister
Locked in barbed Barberton prison
Where people live and die
Spending stabbing days
Entangled nights
In the silent cell of angered bell.

We are proud of you good sister
You whose light bathed the path
Whole-heartedly we tread the trail
Prepared to lay down our lives
For mothers of your mould.

Esther Ka-Maleka the joining spear
A display of seasoning bravery
Pushing forward struggling
Militants born and mothered
Drawing in the fighting milk
That begot them

You dedicated your life
Sacrificed your youth
Living the torture of "solitary" in the crowding of dreams and memories
Alone in the cloud of loneliness
But still the chin up high
For this we honour you

Keep fighting Dorothy keep fighting
Tomorrow we'll stand united
Hand in hand comradely
Holding the dream by the hand
In a liberated South Africa...

NOTES:

- This poem is dedicated to Dorothy Nyembe, who is serving 15 years jail imprisonment. During the Defiance Campaign she served two prison sentences, and in 1956 lead the Natal contingent of women to the Union Buildings in Pretoria. She is due for release in 1984.

The South African regime banned her
Phyllis Altman

I would not mute accept their sacraments
No oil to seal my lips my mind my eyes my heart.

So they tore out my tongue and crippled my hand
Gave me dumb silence as penance
Desolate days to number my rosary
My home my cell, removed from the world of men.

Yet, hidden here
I breathe I think I live I love
That love my solace – the love they hate

It's I who love and they who hate
But I am infinite

Forget not our mothers
Ilva Mackay

Forget not our mothers
awaiting us with an assured patience

Forget not our fathers
languishing in jails
toiling in mines

Forget not our children
lying dead
    dying on the streets

Fists of fury reach out
as we re-affirm:
Africa shall be free!
We shall free her!

OUR MEN WHO FOUGHT
AND DIED AND FIGHT

I honour you all
Mpho Segomotso Dombo

Let there be peace
Where you lie chief
Brave Luthuli in the rich soil
Of the just

Let the evergreen spirit on
The spirit of revolution
To burn in the sinewy hearts
Of the sons and daughters
On the labouring soil

You are honoured
You daughters of Africa
You whose wombs begot soldiers
Plodding the patriotic path
Of mother Africa

I honour you Duma Nokwe, Uncle J.B.
I honour you Mandela, Sisulu, Mlangeni
You whose minds shaped power
Plotting the maps of change
Sculptors of tomorrow

Goldberg, Bram Fischer, Kathrada
Are you not men
You whose sacrifice manned
The living soldiers

Peterson
Fallen body
Spirit of manhood
Rising ever to exist

Oh! Spirit of steel
Spirit that volunteers
Come spirit of Africa
Bring freedom in our lifetime
Bring fighting freedom to our lives.

NOTES:
- Albert Luthuli was president of the ANC.
- Duma Nokwe and Uncle J.B. were high-ranking members of the ANC, who both died in exile.
- Bram Fischer was a member of the Communist Party of South Africa, who died while serving life imprisonment.
- Mandela, Sisulu, Mlangeni, Goldberg and Kathrada are South African patriots serving life imprisonment .
- Hector Peterson was the first school child to be killed by police bullets on June 16, 1976.

This path
Rebecca Matlou

Child of the soil
Child of own destiny
Cross this path
Cross the sword
Ride the lions back
Bound on with shoulders high
Sky in heavens light the path
Echoes from this thorny bush guide the way
Luthuli, Kotane, Mandela, Sisulu trod this path
Pull hard, hack the prickly shrubs
Burden beads on your brow
Pilgrim yoke on your back
Will balm the people's tortured heart
And bid the sod to seed freedom

For prof
Baleka Kgositsile

There are cysts
trying to grow into a cancer
in the womb
whose fertility
was endorsed in red
SOWETO
but I heard
Uncle J.B. Malome Duma
Your troubled lips knew their immortality

This is not cancer
the giant in your small body tells us
when we are haunted by nightmares
Marks speaks to us
when our bodies crumble
our eyes deluded
by mountains of foam
Malome awakens us
This is not Kilimanjaro
Duma lives to show
it is not to be unexpected

Ours is to fight
our last footprints
on the soil of our land say it
no flesh has a right over us
Qiniselani!

the blood on our land speaks
ignore the eye
that does not see itself in
Qiniselani!

NOTES:
- "Quiniselani": "gird yourself for battle, intensify the struggle".
- J.B. Marks, Malome Moses Kotane, and Duma Nokwe were patriots who died in exile.

Gone "forever"
Gloria Nkadimeng

– Last tribute to our esteemed Comrade Moses Kotane

He who made the sun shine upon the oppressed
    is gone...
    and it is forever
    in the flesh
He who uttered those brave words into thirsty ears
    is gone...
    and it is forever
    into earth
He who was leading us down to the valley of freedom
This knight in shining armour
This natural phenomenon this monster
    death has taken him from our parched eyes
    not our hearts
    he is gone...
    and it is forever
Brave he was amongst the bravest
This gem that sparked in the hands of this nation
    but now he is gone...
    and it is forever
    from our eyes
Let us all, clenched fist in clenched fist, therefore for a moment, bouquet his
coffin, now
    with revolutionary songs
    for new
    moment forever

Vuyisile Mini
Rebecca Matlou

Vigorous stalwart
Unshaken by winds of oppression
Yielding not to bitter days
In the dungeon heart of grim death
Sang Mini the language of freedom
Inseparable from warm sounds redeeming
Lays his note in the bars of prison
Ever accepted by his people

Mini man of change
Indispensable to the starved nation
Narrated tales of truth
"Indoda Emnyama Velevutha".
The enemy in his own prison
Challenging
in music
"Basoba!"
Sings the vigour in the heart cell
Sings the valour
Of Mini.

NOTES:
- Vuyisile Mini was a trade union man, a founding member of SACTU.
- "Indoda Emnyama Velvutha": "There comes the black man, Verwoerd".
- "Basoba": "Watch out, he's gonna get you." These are words from Mini's own compositions, prior to being assassinated by the fascist regime.

For Duma Nokwe
Baleka Kgositsile

so many suns
so many moons
so many hopes
so many lives
son of a woman
you have been
and you will be

what is this blindness
and fumbling again and again

can it be that the enemy looming
from where he decrees his schemes
is bent in having an ominous cloud accompanying you everywhere
can it be that the enemy is much nearer
than we think
can it be that we refuse to recognise
his stinking presence
that confuses us
deafens us
blinds us
that we do not heed the repeated cries
of the best of the sons and daughters of our land

is it the inevitable path of the revolution
that the cruel wheels at work day and night
try to grind our best to nothingness all the time
problems problems anxiety

solutions yes
to all of them too
none too unimportant or insurmountable
even though some of us would rather
shelve them until later

yes isolation
in a world full of people
alone on a hospital bed
your mind cannot afford to relax
with pen on paper
you grapple with how to push this point and that
we don't have all the time in the world

son of a million mothers
father of the children of our land
redeemer of enemy tools
great enemy of enemies of mankind
those who have eyes saw how
the vicious wheels tried to crush you
but there is so much of you
that even in a billion years
your granite strength
humble unapologetic tempered
in the furnace of struggle
to split the skies with liberation songs
will remain flowering on this planet...
in all those many lives that shall be stars
that will be many suns
so many moons.

Duma Nokwe (The great leader of South Africa)
Fezeka Makonese

On receiving the news
That the great leader of South Africa
Duma Nokwe had stepped down and entered history
I went high and stood on rocks
Driven by sorrow and grief
Nothing could make me understand
Nor accept the fact
I dragged myself from rock to rock
And I saw trees crowding trees
Hills over hills
A surging scene at a distance

The sweet birds' songs became a hollow sound
The breeze murmured something meaninglessly
I moved on in a low and languid mood
Filled with thoughts of the heart
My eyes swam in tears
All the view from the rocks
Became feeble; dimmed and departed
Like a dream
And I remained with my memories
My sorrows and grief
Indeed tragedy hung over South Africa
Duma Nokwe the beloved son of Africa
The militant of the great revolution
Was no longer in flesh nor in blood
Alas; death is bound to happen
Human life is limited

I murmured to myself
Who will replace him?
Searching for an answer
I gazed into space with the vacant eyes
Of a cow in the field disturbed while grazing
But there was no one to answer
None! None! None at all!

The rocks around me seemed to be
Asking the same question
Who will replace him?
Indeed the loss was great

Duma Nokwe the being we was
is and still remains
For he is one of the discoverers of the road
To freedom and justice
He became the sparkling light
Which will never die.
Before his grave all lovers of
Peace, justice and liberty
Will bow as a token of honour

His social life
Like a deep-rooted tree
With branches covering a large space
With delicious fruits
Offered indiscriminately
Among the nations
His fair-mindedness in
judgment

His simplicity, generosity and
Kindness
A tireless militant leader
Ever affectionate

Duma Nokwe though you stepped down
The strong impact you left
On the destiny of liberty –
Dignity
Will remain in us forever
And we will bow
To your grave as a token
Of honour.

Oliver Waka Tambo
Rebecca Matlou

O liver Tambo

L ife born grass-roots greenery

I nto the wombs of this country this earth

V ery sharp to answer the call that wakes

E ndure you child of fists and spears to

R end and re-shape the mains of these mounds

land that now bears mounds of death.

T ell all the gods those old types of our will

A ll is set now: the army bright eyed, tall

M an to man moulded in mortar that gave you birth now again

B ending the earlier spears into bright sickles on the shoulders of our new nation

O h soldier wait to harvest ripeness; husband man celebrate our birth

BLACK GREEN AND GOLD...

My country
Zinziswa Mandela

– For Mandela

I stand by the gate
School's out
Smoke fills the location
Tears come to my eyes

I wipe them away
I walk into the kitchen
To see my mother's
Black hard-washing hands
A forceful smile from
A tired face

We sit and have supper
I pick up a picture of
My father and look
My mother turns away
Tries to hide

My father left my mother
In his arms
He is roughly separated
From her

The van pulls away
Mother watches bravely enough
I as a child do
Not understand
My heart aches
How I long to see my father
At least to hold his hand
And comfort him
Or at least to tell him
He'll be back some day.

Mandela and all comrades in prison
Ilva Mackay

You are just number 466/64 to them
sweeping dusty paths,
tilling and raking the soil of that island.

But you are the strength,
the determination
that flows through the veins of your children
fighting for you,
    you and all those numbers.

Yes, with your space firmly in your hand
    till and take the soil Mandela
like your brothers, sisters, sons and daughters
who toil and sweat for Africa

She is ours
we too shall know no rest
till she comes back to us.

Spearhead
Baleka Kgositsile

Tense
we like a jigsaw puzzle
Intense
the life we filter into us
Intensify
is the clarion call
this year of the Spear
Solomon here we come
child and parent of our dignity
here we come

Solomon Mahlangu (Addressing his jailers)
Rebecca Matlou

Don't be puzzled that I smile
even in moments of anguish
don't be sullen that I keep my spine
upright
in this grim den
in this intended grave
I am a free man
in your leper camp
I remain a full man
do not question then my distant gaze
my stare goring instant bloodless walls
is born of moving truths I've lived

This stream,
fountain of life
this gathered storm I am
born of uncertainty's nausea
bearing thorns which prick my soul
your cold torture which seeks
to steal my being
steeled it days ago
chilling suspense
once seemed to crack my brain
your lawless claws
still kill our unborn babes
you joy to bend us to endless humiliation
ANIMAL DEATH!

This stream
this tapped fountain of life
weaned gathered storm of hardship
born of nauseating uncertainty
bears thorns which prick my soul
cold torture
which steels my being
chilling suspense
that cracks my brain
your lawless claws
kill unborn babies
you joy to bend us to endless humiliation
ANIMAL DEATH!

But as you grope corners
for borrowed peace and purse
I offer my people echoes of happiness
you who curfew your minds
with your backs to the prison wall
cradle it until you stoop
until it drills your chest
until you bow to melt
into broken pieces of hope
bow to fate
hold its quivering tale
(to you I say)
I touch this darkness and give it meaning.

NOTES:
- Solomon Mahlangu was murdered by the fascist regime on 6 April 1979, despite concerted international appeals against the death sentence.

Solomon Mahlangu (Child of the revolution)
Gloria Mtungwa

Serving the cause
of justice
you've triumphed
fascist contemplation you spin
you have spun
the wheel of revolution
you've striven courageously ahead

You stand unwavering
in the face of racist brutality
their knees quivering
in fearful anxiety
while the nation prides itself within
in your dedication
honour, and stability
to the cause of
LIBERTY

Back unbending
face brightly smiling
defiantly, mockingly
braving the storm
of ferocious death

SUBMISSION
a word non-existent
in your mind
TORTURE
a cruel joy to your all steeled body and your soul unstolen
VICTORY
a capital-letter word
for all your woes

Jeer and laugh comrade
at their evil
futile technicalities
MK is on its way
to glorify
your sacrifice
and grind the fascist wheel
to smithereens in the smithies of the nation wholly new.

Solomon my brother
Lindiwe Mabuza

Where does brave steel go
When it has firmed foundations
Stood erect crippling infirmity
Then blazed across furious skies
Sharply tracing revolution's flowers
With crimson tips
Along the rough edges of history
Say where does burnished steel go?

Where can Mahlangu go
When banned he has faced
Death row teeth
Those razor-blade projections drooled
To grotesque our peoplehood
Down in the living inferno
Where he has heard hell's clawed
Deafening rumble
Yet also seen open trap-doors
Leading to the dangled dazzle
Of silver and gold and diamonds
All his for a traitor's song
But the warrior spit courage voluminous
Direct into the devil's face
Say where can our comrade go?

Mahlangu cannot else go
Save forward to the front line
Where consciousness climbs all storms
When the brilliance of his young life
Sparks inside a million hearts
The soldier triumphs
Where together we build steady forts
To break adversity
When together we womb the dream to birth

Mahlangu cannot else
But fuse with seasons
That disperse armed seeds into positions
Warmed with martyrs' sacrifice
On lonely cold nights he vigils
Midst hungry watchful eyes
In the dark night of crafty enemy flights
Then breakfasts with battalions
On vengeance defiance and dare

Didn't you see him today
Even right now
Present us his will
That last testament
Signed with blood
Pure from the flame of Vuyisile Mini
Moving like the gaze of Bram Fischer

Didn't you hear him today
Even right now
Sing his poem of love
Write an epitaph of love
with LIFE
"My blood will nourish the tree
Which will bear the fruits of freedom" he said

Yes Mahlangu unbending
Is the MK's symphony
Never reported in enemy press
He is you and I everywhere
Completing his interrupted walk to freedom

Yes for him too with LIFE
We must reach freedom's rich estates...
Marching
To the unbroken rhythm
Of surging dancing spears

PHASES OF STRUGGLE:
RESOLUTION, EXILE, PERSPECTIVE, LOVE, CALL TO JUSTICE AND ARMS

To be young
Jeanette Solwandle

To be young
    Fighting to be free,
Nothing else before but Motherland, South Africa
    Yes
To be young

To be everywhere young
    Awake to the slings and spikes
Of racism, fascism, apartheid
    To be still young and growing

To be young and then
    Feel freedom hunger
Deep enough in the furious depths
    Young to defy boundaries then
Stretch and fling wide the future
    Young to say yes and vow
My blood for you rich soil

Yes to be young
    To simply say
I want this need called freedom
    In mountains and valleys
In cities and dorps
    I will fight in my own South Africa
Till victory bounces and resounds
Away from the hands of begging fascists

Yes to be young enough
    To dream and build heavens
Down here on this earth.

Hope
Phumzile Zulu

Son of Africa don't lament
Your mother and father
Have not abandoned you
Your home should not frustrate
You are indigent they say
But your poverty is man-made and temporary
For your education
We will work till the blood in our veins runs no more
For your life and our country
We will fight till the sinews in our bodies seize all weariness fatigue and
ceasing

Stand firm
Son of Africa don't lament
Hope
     Son of Africa
     Be assured of final victory
     Hope... and fight forward

Exile blues
Baleka Kgositsile

let them roll
let the blues roll out
but "this load is heavy it requires men"
has nothing to do with baritone or beard
it is a word of warning wisdom
when the uncontrollable miles
between you and home
the beautiful land
you vowed to liberate
become unbearable
and you ask yourself
if it was worth your leaving the loved ones
as if you left home
a victim of a stupor
when having been rejected
like vomit from a stomach
you try to examine
if it is the food that is stale
or the stomach that is sick
when you are threatened by paralysis
in the midst of so much to be done
when the pettiness has played so many games with you
that like an addict
you do not remember when you did not crave
just another piece of gossip

when the demon trinity
inferiority complex
self assertion
sadism
have become your masters
that you put the stamp
on your own death certificate
as you try to destroy
when you drink yourself insensible
into the gaping dark void
that is ready like the vicious jaws
of a shark to receive you
when some other comrades have fallen victim
to mental breakdown
and you shudder wondering
if you won't be next to be ambushed
when you make a habit of exchanging blows
that should be kept for the enemy
when you feel trapped
suffocating cornered
at a cul-de-sac
and your tears roll down uncontrollably
as memories invade you daily
maybe let them roll
let them blues roll out
let them roll out the blues
till oblivion sneaks to your rescue

when later you feel lighter
retrieve the zeal that made you leave home
lest you go down the drain
with the stinking rot of history
when the song goes
"this load is heavy it requires men"
that has nothing to do with baritone or beard
it is a word of wisdom and warning
that our history is so reddened
with the blood of the best of our land
even the enemy gets more vicious by the second
because the enemy also knows
"victory is certain!"
is not an empty slogan

It takes a heart
Jumaimah Motaung

Can you imagine... how much it takes to realise the atrocities, maimings and outright murders committed by Vorster and Botha's Gestapo? It really takes a heart!

One could relax and sit back and perhaps say: Vorster will pay for his crimes. But one thing I absolutely know... perpetual pain and pressure cannot be tolerated forever. Remember Vietnam, Angola, Ethiopia and struggles long before!

Come witness what Verwoerd has done!
Giants imprisoned
Others sent to the gallows
Full-blooded sons and daughters buried alive?
Such overkill to satisfy insatiable greed?
It really takes a heart.
Desperate to nip
Revolutionary buds
To fell forever our tallest trees...
But it was not to be

What person could forsake the little already collected under the very oppressive system? It really takes a heart.
What person could withstand all those abuses tortures solitary confinements, detentions without trials? Who can?
It takes a heart.

Who can?
The very ones in Robben Island
Caged in John Vorster Square
In Modderbee...
The stand they have taken, firm.
It is like climbing a perilous mountain,
Like swimming across a far stretched ocean,
Where death lurks in every wave
In every cave
And even on the spray

You might thing it risk, you who do not know what oppression is.
You might even thing people crazy to stand against a country so strong! But
one thing is certain...
no matter how hard a rock, chipping it every day will undoubtedly bring it down.
No matter how tall. No matter how long. And... yes, I agree: fascist South Africa
is strong, militarily built up by Western monopolies.

Some hardware: France — helicopters, armoured vehicles
                   USA — warships, multipurpose monoplanes
                   FRG — helicopters, tanks, nuclear schemes
                   Britain — armoured vehicles, warships
                   et cetera et cetera et cetera

Because of this,
Patriots will forsake degrees
Children their everything
Teaching the world to know
They do not care
For petals in the hand
Hot with the itch for the spear
They do not care
For luxuries to dazzle the sight
It really takes a heart.
It takes our heart.

To Zambia
Lindiwe Mabuza

Zambia
Coppertone Zambezi lands
Zambia rich vastness
Like a woman heavy
With the weight of birth life
And all her unknown pleasures

Manchild Zambia
Waiting for the people
The only midwives of all treasures
Thirsting for their love
To deliver Zambia
Bouncing child of seasoned years
Here you are
Mounting the zigzag hills of progress
Often with piercing pain
To those serene heights and peaks
Where the lush promise of independence resides

Zambia
Warm, always getting warmer
Mother, daughter and sister
Of twin liberty-bound enslaved Zimbabwe
You truly Central Africa,
Look at the roaring thunder unleashed
Of your Zambezi
Charging towards barbed-wire fences
And polluted regions of the burning South
Hold on Zambia!
Copperbelt of fertility

Not for labour's relief and comfort only
Are you central
Above the wastelands of racism and fascism
For on your tender shoulders and growing back
Fall and centre hot questions
Whose answers
Will tighten to untighten
Those lower parts

Zambia
Open gateway to the freedom fighters' dream –
The dream...
Thoughts of gold
Diamond hopes
A Mozambique march
The determination
The resilience of Angola –
The dream...
To your peace-loving land-locked harbours
These the fighters bring
Before your caring vigilance they grow
Nourished by the food of all patriots
The sense of history
The certainty of victory
Zambia
It is on your shores
That we world our pain
It is here
Where the fighters' dream
Indelible on the minds and wills
Is purged, forged
Into the solid whiz of a bullet

Then taken home to battle
There to burst
Into the glorious star of FREEDOM!

Zambia
Magnanimous bronze sun baked mosaic people
Varied in tongue
As the succulent abundance
Of all your loving seasons
When they teach the world
The art of giving...
And you Zambia
You the embracing people of all Africa
While we patiently wait
Burnishing in your workshop
With you, with us
Sharper and undiverted should our SPEARS strike
Those chameleon-like foxes
The enemies of true humanism

For humanism is not a word
Is not a change in name
But revolves from the inside of things
And a way of life
It is not yesterday, not today
But the best of both
Sifted and shaped into
Immune foundations for the future
Whose embryo is conceived
In yesterday and today's fight
Against the exploitation of man by man

For humanism is not souvenir photographs
In black and white
Nor is it Technicolor tokens, pacifiers, dummies
Stuffed to muffle sounds of need
From the growling bellies of poverty
From the watergates of Kanyama
But humanism banishes hunger from the base
For the base –
The wanting victims of pillage and theft –
It establishes equality between
The bricklayer and the steering guide –
The worker's choice

Humanism is
Zambia
Your gift of life...
Already you donate blood
To water new lands being prepared
In the talking bullet zones
Like inland oceans
Your Secheke Martyrs' blood
Will not cease their Southward journey
Until revolutionary storms have rocked the Cape
Into harbours of good hope.
Humanism is
Your unknown soldier's precious life
Now mingling with Moyo Dube Mangena
And like arteries from the heart of Africa
Tributaries gush towards Namibia
Then converge on all Southern fields

Zambia
It must be along your steaming Zambezi
That we shall gather again
After the day of reckoning
With its war dances and hallelujahs
To erect monuments
Of those unsafe ones
In the stomach of vultures
Zambia
It must be here
We shall shape tombs, landmarks
The battlefields will be harvest fields aplenty
Libraries will be wombs of the mind
And museums breathing
Hospitals schools history gyrating with life
Now made a luxury
By this capitalist sacrilege
Of barbed-wire bandits and boundaries
We shall leave mother, home
But for the things you've done for us
Over and over
Thank you
Zambia

NOTES:
- Kanyama is a poor section of Lusaka declared a disaster area after devastating floods in 1978.
- Secheke is a place in Zambia where, on the pretext of pursuing ZAPU guerillas, Ian Smith's bandits killed Zambian nationals.
- Moyo Dube Mangena was a Zimbabwe freedom fighter, murdered by the enemy in exile.

Swim comrade
Rebecca Matlou

This swarthy swollen torrent
Vomits you my comrade
You the living alluvium
Plucked by these rhythmic sighs
Hearts drum this instant
Melody of grief and tribulation
Come ashore dear redeemer
Bids the voice of Moshoeshoe
Makana calls mid hazard waves
Swim comrade heal this ulcer –
Your people are waiting...

Flap your sides flow nearer
Freedom waits to meet you
Hold my wing-swim ashore
Let us hold the rolling stream
Together direct this flood of life
Strain voiced in desperate pitch
Swim comrade save "us"
Look homeward now and join this tide

Hush melody murmurs, hand beckons
Waves furrow toward the inevitable message of shores
The relic of the frolic sound echoes
Turbulent streams fond of dreams
Repeatedly bruted comrade you
Our likes pounced yet on prey
Swim across with spotted spear

The crimson rays of dawn
Bless the honour-blood of the shield
No mermaid skill nor acrobat plunge
But webs of unity and love surface and dive
Swim comrades blend with pebbles

Come lest we crumble comrade
The very banks of our being
Swim comrade...
The people are waiting.

What do you say
Baleka Kgositsile

What do you say
when you have
these wings that propel you
to heights and depths
which defy measurement

But this here
this now
is not free
from unhappiness
this here and now
is a postulate pimple
a shiny blister
is a boil

Between these punches
that are our life
out of whirlpool and turmoil
when you drift to the edge
where the sea meets the land
ride on the waves
and let life reclaim you
moving deeper and deeper
ransacking this maze
for every bit of life

To a comrade
Lindiwe Mabuza

oh comrade
we would love less
you and I
if we loved not freedom more

for it was not
in the arena of
spring-propelled coupling
we first met
where feverish blood
erects
roadblocks
for the mind
there where visions
nakedly prostrate
on inverted thorns
of self-indulgence

no comrade though we danced and
bathed in shimmers
of love supreme
in honeyland
comrade
we met not sipping words
methodically
or adding pretty frills
to questions and answers
only to challenge

drab
with gaudiness

yes comrade yes
we met
each voyaging
on the same trans-oceanic plane
we met
all of us cruising
no comrade
we sped
even near pounding shores
rippling
separating
the yeasty radiance
of that widening eastern stage
from the tottering
tatters
darkening the ulcerous west

yes
we grew
too the will
also erected
in the hands of a giant idea
that we agreed
to hold
across all fields
waiting for more hands

we met
oh yes comrade
in the steel arms
of young Soweto
groaning
unarmed
bearing the bullet-frozen weight
of Hector drained
by those who always leave reservoirs
parched
of tomorrow's nectar

there we met again
as brave tears overpowered age
and strolled down children's defiant cheeks
writing anger
indelible
etching
for the world to know the reason
the fight for freedom

comrade
there is no exit
when the sounds of history
curdle our blood
except crossing
over to the unknown knowns
of revolutions
knowable...

let me tell you
about an all-Africa child
I saw:
he was away from pressed
uniforms of schools fenced
away from the praise-poetry
of beaming young soccer-lovers
when they marvel at their peers
chasing defeat
with a ball

comrade
the electric fingers
of this stone-faced manchild
scavenged for his dinner promise
pulling disintegrating navy guts
out of a concoction of bloody dung
stagnant
along the streets of this and any ancient
African city
built in the foundations
of outworn empires
beggar-paved and
over-bargained

but do you remember
when we swayed
from side to packed side
squeezed in buses
that became jungles?
didn't that dry sweat

on tired faces speak?
we never remarked
about the lazy stench
from dilapidated homes of workers
when we negotiated precarious steps
along the edges of putrid canalets
and other festering nests of infant deaths
and then remembered
how the knife of profit
amputates hands
in modern African capitals
and metropoles elsewhere
Oh Chile! Chile! Chile!
Neruda's Chile!
could we but everyday
mould masterpieces
in the laboratories
of many Vietnams!

so yes comrade
we could not love more
to minus freedom
for you and I met
and always will
to forge multiple dawns
of new horizons.

For my comrade
Rebecca Matlou

comrade, i see pain in your face
settled deep below your eyes
i can see your heart bleed pain
your heart bleeds for Africa and the land
blood burns your being
    transcend the flood
sing reed music home
continue to sing sound
with feeling of real you
chill those walls barbed in wire
disturbing the destined road
of the scarred nation bleeding (salt) wounds
    transcend the flood
you are a slave no more to the world
sculpture your wishes
harness the slimy puddle
this wave is harsh
it rocks the boat to limp on stone
the road is slimy the road shakes all
in trembles all it thunders all
    transcend this flood
live sound
leave clear prints of healing on our time.

Agape: Tomorrow
Lindiwe Mabuza

when they seal love
with smiling clusters of diamond
they never tell about the dark depths looming behind

when they say love
is like a red red rose
some never tell about the green thorns guarding the petals

nor can they who remember
fully relish the honeycomb
when the thumb swells blue from all the stings

but in the free and obedient hive of our growing love
worker bees honour
the rose
erect... the brilliance
of the future
partaking of today's dark thorns.

The gulp of unity
Rebecca Matlou

take this it is for love
the methuselah looked at the milky faces
for past memories mistakes and misery
gulp this blood sacred liquid
from this stream well cut the painful past
from this stream well shape our present future
as the debris rolls down the pit of limbo
let's gargle and spit the venomous sputum
this will merge black and white in blood bonds
this then is for forgiveness

the night lay thick and thunderous
the storm poured down and abated
on the old man's head lay imprinted
the genesis of war and peace...
forgive him dear child for having sharpened
and nurtured the poisoned ivy
forgive him child for past dreams
for his dreams were reality raw
your dreams are not defined yet
let him tell the tale and you tear the path
gulp down this blooded sacred liquid
this is for life this is for unity

purge me i say the hysteria hissed
calmly his spirit mounted
as his feeling ascended the past
a shaken voice demanded
hold this knowing hand and knot
i will lead you yonder
to cross the stream of life
and humanity
this night is mine... and yours
this sky we will share... and shield
this is for love and unity
    gulp it... gulp it...
    this is for love
    this is for unity
    this is for love and unity
    gulp it down...

Faces of commitment
Lindiwe Mabuza

It's been long now
I was afraid of writing
About you, us
For you would not want
Such sculpture
To subdue those multitudes
That gave you birth
And armed you with their heroism
Carved from the rock
That is Maluti
Always vigilant over our boisterous waters...
Lekwa Nciba Thukela

But I can write you now
For once again
Although your memory still invades
My weakness
Like close-circuit slow motion pictures
Yet somehow certain I know
Yours is among those thatching spears

It has been with growth
And puzzles
This loneliness
We stretch like tropical green
From stacked thoughts
You organised over the hours
These treasures we all shared

Over thirsty waves
Before the silencing of your voice
But you will not be stilled
For justice cries out for more
And the voices of right
Grow beyond containment
Like love
When it overrules prescription

I awoke
With the thought of you
This morning
You of that land
Where jacarandas scorn
This miscarriage of justice
There where our people
Battle for birth
Where even young will
Defies electrodes' hell
Which gambol the length and depth
Of overstretched swollen bodies
In all the John Vorster Squares

I thought of you comrade
Daring the enemy underground
In the struggles' workshops
There making history flourish
Right there where the enemy's hatchet

Hovers over those who dream
Then step by step build
The greatness of man
Amid the ashes fertilising spring
And the many
Who may never be known
Because accident or trick
May early call
For investment of their fresh blood
Despite decades of streams
That usher in gold-bars
In the miner's hands
And the point-blank murders
Of some with gold dust in their lungs

I thought of you
In the theatre of war
Which all must enter
To find exits to life
Especially because when it broadcasts
And scatters us apart
It also defines precisely
To bind us closer

Old age fund
Susan Lamu

They stand with crooked back
Whole nights;
It is the eve of the great day;
Coming once in six long weeks.

They come from all over to assemble
Overnight
Waiting for the pay-master to come.
Dressed in rags
Shivering in the cold – they make the best of beds
On the sandy ground.

At sunrise grandchildren run along
Black coffee, bittersweet to warm old bones;
To check whether grannies have not dropped – giving up the OLD AGE
FUND to rest forever.

Fifteen hours' patience,
The pay-master appears.
"Is jou boek in orde?"
Before they answer, still struggling to move old lips
The pay-master's impatience turns them back;
Grandchildren back home scrutinise the Book...

The pay-master retires to the White Area
To come after six long, long weeks,
Then the trouble starts!
The Black Jack comes at four in the morning;
"Old girl, the Super wants to see you..."
"Oh *my kind*, the office only opens at eight..."

The Black Jack pulls her by the leg
She has to go and wait for Super...
At fifteen past eight
Granny starts roaming the streets;
She has no place to live.

She could not pay rent in the due day...
The pay-master was gone.
Her book was not in order;
She waited all night,
She has no house.

I can hear the knell tolling,
Granny buried
Shrouded in the gold soil of this motherland
Without a rag: this poverty
This insult of a book
That never was in order.

Open season
Lindiwe Mabuza

After blood-spilling centuries
Decades of trespassing
Seasons of poaching
The uninhibited hunters
Declared open season on African people
Announced wide range opportunities
For trained hunters of children
Turned our stolen fields into hunting grounds
When they brought the game veld
In military hippos
And other death spitting gifts
From Western fellow-poachers
Right to the streets of Soweto
They piled death...

Alexandra
Athlone
Mamelodi
Gugulethu
Langa
The hunters declared
Open season
On June 16 1976

But
In treeless jungles
Garbage cans
And rusty scraps of zinc
Cannot camouflage human prey
Cannot give cover
Against the blazing volley of death
Little school blazers and books
Make poor frail shields
When blood-thirst hunters
Want human trophies
And our young become prime venison
For frothing beasts of capital and race
When the bullet-clawed ones
Prowl by day
"Seeking whom to devour"
On the fenced streets of our cities
Where gold grows multifold
And people into mine dumps

We are cornered in the fight-back
We want out of the confining cage
We want destruction of these game reserves
But in their crave for tenderest flesh
They run amock
Their rabies infected hounds of profit
To crunch every crash resistant bone
In our fierce pack
This unconquerable do or die youth
On the day of the hyena
When the fascist sportsman
Who never hunts from hunger

But murders for fun game and greed
Unleashed war on infants
After kicks on his backside
On the battlefield of Angola
The brazen coward declared
Open season

Oh our mangled bodies abused
Still breathing against repression
Were cast into gluttonous game reserves
Our young were hurled into lions' dens
At Kruger National Park
Bet even lions can only stare aghast
At such beastly carnage
Such wanton waste
Overfed with fresh human steak
They only sniffed and snort
At the latest black cargo
Then shake that bewildered mane
Walk away
Fondly teasing
Their playful cubs
And we remember those born free
In boer-protected homes
Where "civilised" head hunters
Make game of our people

What would a green mamba do
What would this or that snake do
In branchless reserves of cheap labour
These fertile gardens
Of dead labour?

What wouldn't all the vipers do
With all these bullet-loaded bodies?
The green mamba would only twist
Perhaps coil his agile body in shock
Maybe he would only slither away
Sensing there would be other frames
Sensing there would be other times
When the hunter will be back
To extract more life out of the oppressed
The happy mamba will slide away
Feeling in every nerve
There would be more human sacrifice
For all crawling creatures
To empty their last venomous dregs
When open season is declared
On our dear land
Its beautiful people

But no
Listen to the roar of the drums
The very horizons swims in the thud
Thundering that deep-grown anger
Do you see vengeance ambush apartheid
There where determination mirages ancestral faces
Where freedom out-manoeuvres baaskap infirmity
And ISANDLWANA flashes across the sky
Right here where we hear new footsteps
Hymns of dare rising from us the people
Rising from Angola's red soil
"A snake's bite is cured
With the snake's poison"

Wembube! Wembube! Wembube!
Songs of hunt assuring
Songs that wed the will
To the language of the dance of spears
Pierce your strains
Rain from Maluti mountain tops
tips safely land deep
In racist heartlands
And the feathers quiver the warriors oath
On these same hunting grounds
These blood stained greedy gangs
Will be hunters no more
For they are the tracked one trapped
The cornered quarry
In pandemonium fury
Bash those granite heads
From corner to spear-headed inch
Scattered their blindfolded minds
As we declare open season
On the marauding monster
For the African National Congress of South Africa
Lives to tower everyday
Watered by our blood
The salt lakes of pain

Mandela Goldberg Kathrada Mbeki
Mlangeni Mhlanga Motsoaledi Sisulu
Still hammer with heads erect to stars
Heed their life-giving spirit
Let that Mkhonto bearing arm rise
Spread into an impenetrable forest

Of gun powder and lead

Comrades hold the hungry point

To Apartheid's jugular vein

Deepen our sharpened thrust

On throats that bellow mind devouring discords

Close rank spears

Slid open the infectious belly of oppression

Man woman child

Descend for our ascent

Direct freedom's appetite

To where only bravery can celebrate

Unstring the heart

Pull out the poisoned womb

For vultures to satiate on

Till peoples' just hopes volcano

Because the hunters of justice

Live and grow everyday

Then a united people

A victorious nation

A triumphant world

Will refrain songs of peace

Over distant heights

Call lovers of the sun to stretch out

Hoist the faithful shield

BLACK GREEN GOLD

A beacon to all hunters of the future

To pause and just for a little while

Drink from our living springs

Springs to drown deserts of injustice

Springs to re-dress our raped land

Fountains sprouting sparkling seeds
On prostituted justice
Yes these will be springs
Where little children of Soweto
Mamelodi Mashu Langa Athlone
Can drink wash or just simply
SPLASH
And like tadpoles
Freely swim
On all June sixteens to come

Fascism strikes again
Fezeka Makonese

It is not long ago when fascism
In South Africa
Swallowed our heroes in Sharpeville
It is not so long ago when racialism
Buried our heroes
Alive at Coalbrook
Women were widowed
Children unfathered
Today racialism has again shamelessly
Mowed our children down
With NATO arms
At Soweto
In Bulhoek

Racialism! Fascism! Imperialism!
Your days are numbered on African soil
You have committed crimes enough
Never to be forgotten
You have killed
You have robbed
You have drained the wealth of our continent
You deserve death

Imperialism, your kingdom is falling apart
Your grave has been made
Days fixed when you'll be
Driven fast to your abyss
Mother Africa has condemned you to death

You are mad: and I mean it
Phumzile Zulu

What did you mean when you called me benighted
Savage pagan barbarian
You must have been mad
I know now
I say it and I mean it

When you found me here in Africa
You said I was hungry
You came carrying a big book called "BIBLE"
And you called yourself "missionary"

You were going to offer
Food for my life
But to my surprise
Never was I hungry like this before

Instead of bread you gave crumbs
Maybe you just want me to salivate
Why do you act like this
Fat controlling experimenter
Who at the beginning called himself "Good SAMARITAN"

I have realised that you did not mean all that good
You had come here to explore my wealth
Bloody spy in camouflage of a missionary
Did you think you would succeed forever and ever?

Look here ...

Now that you are aware
That I am hard to get
You try and play monkey tricks
But you have failed with your BANTU EDUCATION
You thought I would bow down till when?

You stole my forefathers' land
You thought I would bow down till when? ... Huh!
I mean it
And I mean it
I am going to stand your lie
You found me comfortable
You requested that I give you fresh water and vegetables
And at the end my blood has become your water
My body your vegetables
I have given a hand
But now you want the whole arm
You are not going to get me
And I mean it!

You tell me you are going to give me scattered portions
Of my own soil
And now you claim that this is a white man's country
You forget how you came here
You are a fool
You are mad
And I mean it!

No more words now
Lerato Kumalo

I get your point precise
lady, gentleman of the world
you say you know
apartheid is a crime against
humanity
and you are part of it

I realise your argument
that it is certainly indefensible
to give approximately 87% of our country
to about 13% of the population
that originally came from
where
you unfortunately are part of

I read but scorn your logic though
that violence begets violence
when you supply guns and money
to those who had them, have had them and have them,
that two wrongs don't make a right
when countless times
you veto my freedom
at the United Nations
that diplomacy works wonders
when you fatten on the blood of my people
in that part of the
world
you unfortunately are part of

But my point argument and logic
come
from piles of dead bodies
and the necks struggling under the yoke
ask them what they think of me
"a nice girl like you" as you put it
when I shoulder with pride
this AK-47
ask what they think of you
and your cocktail party wisdom
"a nice person like you"

No more words now
till our Nuremberg trials
judge the rallies
and weigh Munich

We demand punishment
Sono Molefe

– For a great teacher, Pablo Neruda

We need not tell you,
you the new and brave old ones:
no, we need not tell you,
about all these screaming deeds of butchery;
you, the unconquered millions
of our prostituted, crucified land:
we would not add another burden
to your memory weighted down already
by silent movies
of the disemboweling of our country, our South Africa

No, fellow suffering fighters, compatriots, we would not invite you
to this passing of a verdict on the murderers
still at large all over the country
no, we would not call on you
to bear witness except...
except that the time is ripe
for justice to take control,
for us – you and I, we the people –
to demand punishment;
for all the atrocities
committed by the worshippers of
silver and gold against us

WE DEMAND PUNISHMENT

We could show you
what the monster's paws left
criss-crossed deep
all down the outstretched limbs and spine
of our bleeding country –
these bleeding marks
will never naturally heal into scars
because fascists always strike on raw wounds
because of renewed daily whippings
on our bare backs, black and blue
these marks gape and stare
for all the world to see and taste
the bitter dregs of fascism

Oh yes countrymen
come close and look on the marks on this body
let us approach these wounds country-wide open
these wounds so wise all seeing
like all the unshut eyes of our children
whose innocence was mined with bullets
mid-air Soweto streets
the same that are playgrounds for workers children
come let's dip deep our fingers in the wounds steep them
and across the high wailing skies of our wills
write
for the whole world to know

                                    WE DEMAND PUNISHMENT

We demand punishment
for death by murder
when little bits of brain matter
were left to shrivel up on gravel and sand
across a head that the brain should not have left
we must punish

Remember the bloody potholes
still overflowing all over South Africa
where their depth defies
the ever roaming funnel of howling winds
those chamber-maids of capitalism
when they attempt to suck and cover-up
the true source of these scarlet flames of fascism
this galloping reign of terror

WE DEMAND PUNISHMENT

You must remember all of them
all our dead yes you must
they had names like yours
Mini Loza February Molefe Motaung Khangile
Fischer Mohapi Mdluli Saloojee Mahlagu Ngqabi
ordinary names like your surnames –
in Alexandra Witbank Glencoe Ladysmith
In Port Elizabeth De Aar
you too Kimberley and Bloemfontein Dimbaza
haven't you seen endless ready graves?
do you ever see them open-mouthed in white-Durban
Cape Town Kroonstad or Benoni?

others have been murdered
gold-miners farmworkers machinists
people with jobs like yours –
what of Mini, Vuyisile Mini?
he was for all those who work
then they accused him of murder
Mini burst into song
as the fascist thugs led him to the gallows –
that unbreakable torchbearer among workers
struggling against capitalism
the exploitation of man by man...

WE DEMAND PUNISHMENT

CAPITALISM we want punished
for every drop of sweat
which mingles with our blood
to give muscle and sinew
to hounds and parasites of profits

WE DEMAND PUNISHMENT

For breaking our backs
Bending over our own stolen land
And for our hands forced to bleed treasures
Out of our agonised motherland

WE DEMAND PUNISHMENT

Capitalism we must punish
for every brick of gold we bring forth
for every fruit we bring forth
every box we pack to send overseas
give sweet nectar
to the gluttonous throats of blood-suckers
bringing us closer to the edge of the abyss

WE DEMAND PUNISHMENT

Not one not ten not thousands
but millions of us workers
place before parasites everyday
mountains of profit
before the banquet for bosses
even as our children's hollow lives
stretch the little ribs and stomach
with malnutrition

WE DEMAND PUNISHMENT

Twenty four hours a day
every capitalist law whips us into line
laws steal our wealth and strength
for Oppenheimers' dynasty to stretch
from Johannesburg to Tel Aviv to New York, Yokohama, Rio de Janeiro…
we give and give and give and die giving
they take and take and take and increase and multiply
taking and

WE DEMAND PUNISHMENT

INTERNATIONAL IMPERIALISM must be punished
the fat sharks, United States, Japan, Britain, and all the killer sharks of the world
have all cast lots over our wealth;
checkerboard patterns of greed
dishonour our land;
all over the country
their names are flashed before us
they dance and grin before our eyes
laughing at the poverty they leave behind...
like pigs the gorge themselves to bursting point
with your rights and ours
only to disgorge the profits
at the welcome tables of
Rockefeller's Chase Manhattan Bank
Ford Motors Anglo-American
General Electric General Motors
Afrocs Stewarts and Lloyds
ICI SKF ITT
SHELL Toyota Krupp

All around us they are
look around and see them
the brand names that have agreed
to brand us slaves in our country
behind the shadows of the boers
for them we demand not one
but multiple doses of pain
to be injected on this massive jaw
of international imperialism that masticates masses of humanity
this reason
this root of Apartheid

WE DEMAND PUNISHMENT

for the source of all our ills
the people must punish them

Brave ones sons daughters of history
a proud and tall history
a history rising above
the strains and stench of racism:
brave ones we need not remind you
of the meaning of our colour
of the cross-curse of our colour
of the excuse of our colour
how they pile all their evil
on the colour of our skin
They suck us dry for their profits
then point at our skin for a reason
sweeter than the white workers blood
our blood sustains the parasite
the parasite rewards the white worker more
and points at our skin for a reason
the gluttonous businessman
makes holy and everlasting
this man-made crime of hoarding
and points at our
skin for reason

They take white people and wish them a white-wash
they will turn them into a nation of fools
they will mix them up with a few black-sheep
they will feed all on lies and tricks
and some tales about white goodness
they will hate our colour

also because of what they lack
constantly they reword the neon signs
that invite more blood donors
to charge the veins and arteries of capitalism
The bosses will love our blood more
the more the white fold hates us
creating a rift among those who work
black and white

We need not remind you countrymen
how exploitation then and now
always multiplies in our darkness
drinking red blood of the muscled heart that works whatever colour the skin
black or white or yellow or brown drinking in the dark red blood to make
whose bodies whole and rich
But we must make all the rich those so flesh-fever rich
take and swallow this shark-size punishment
when workers' hands ply to render sterile
the womb of devouring systems
always cunningly filled
without the slightest drop of sweat
always overflowing with our blood
and see no crime in that

                                          WE DEMAND PUNISHMENT

Ovens of terror unleash their flames
when orders to shoot to kill rampage our land
find only children
only singing for justice
when Nazi eyes turn their wheels of madness
to devour enemies of Apartheid
they roll with swastika points
For the old guards of capitalism
the wayfarers of injustice
whose names
we dare not forget
when the trumpet for justice calls
demanding vengeance
for crimes against humanity
committed every minute by
Kruger, Vorster, Botha, Malan
Koornhof, Van der Berg, Visser
Geldenhuys, David Kriel
Boss, Dons
No less than the poison brewed for us
Such punishment these deserve and more

AND MORE PUNISHMENT FOR

GENOCIDE . . . . the mass executions of our people

WE DEMAND PUNISHMENT

In the name of the
dead of long ago
in the name of those
they felled
for the dead of
Dimbaza Sharpeville
Bonteheuwel Soweto
Carletonville Athlone

For the ones who stenched our fatherland
with our own blood in the name of those staunch ones
whose blood stanched our wounds – for all

WE DEMAND PUNISHMENT

AND MORE PUNISHMENT FOR

GENOCIDE . . . . the killing of our people because they are

WE DEMAND PUNISHMENT

For those who die in the mines
their slow death from gold dust
their quick death in needless disasters
and the greed of bloodsuckers
For the many whose graves won't be
never ever

WE DEMAND PUNISHMENT

AND MORE PUNISHMENT FOR

GENOCIDE . . . . the naked slaughter of our people

WE DEMAND PUNISHMENT

How many more must be maimed in industry
come now tell us how many?
how many and who
must donate a leg here and a hand there
an eye of just simply flesh
to the cold calculations of profit?
2 000 murdered at work every year
reduces us every year!
50 000 maimed permanently every year
lessens our vigour every year
for all these and other numbers
WE DEMAND PUNISHMENT

AND MORE PUNISHMENT FOR
GENOCIDE .... The deliberate poisoning of our
children's minds
WE DEMAND PUNISHMENT

They plan to shrink our thoughts
they want our mind to swell
from the malnutrition of inferior education
and when we say no
to poison in the language in the whole stack
they stuff our children dead
with bullets and
WE DEMAND PUNISHMENT

For the school children
who have to eat old newspaper
just to quiet the hunger pains
WE DEMAND PUNISHMENT

They swallow up our culture
mix it up with some of their notes
sell it in Europe and USA
where mbube and wimoweh

sound the same
WE DEMAND PUNISHMENT

Who makes profits for nothing every year
is it the sick and starving composer
or the owners of Gallo?
WHO?

They plan and study
the corruption of our culture
distort it and in its place
an array of fads and fashion
sold with every purchase of capitalism
WE DEMAND PUNISHMENT

GENOCIDE . . . . The butchery of our people

The traitors accuse us of treason
detain us for their fun
We hang from prison windows
we commit suicide after death
our mangled bodies die from fasting
and we drown
in buckets of fascistic laughter. . .
in little prison cells
and the crunch of our skulls
on concrete pavements

eight floors down
assures some fascist promotion
like disease injected into a sound body
WE MUST HAVE THEM PUNISHED

They say kaffirs make good manure
when they murder us
fertilise mine dumps
and boer farms and agribusiness
so that potatoes can grow
and multiply in our stead
For the lost and never found
victims of pass laws
for the nerves charged
the raids chasing us like rats
trials endless without passes
foreigned in our own country
countrymen patriots
WE DEMAND PUNISHMENT

GENOCIDE . . . . For the conscious extermination
of our dear people
WE DEMAND PUNISHMENT

We cannot forgive the enemies
we cannot excuse the murders
WE MUST HAVE OUR TRIALS
Have you heard of those "fertilisers"
they injected in our people
eMseleni in Northern Natal?
And when chemicals
begin to work on our starved bodies

every cell in the body
every bone shrinks
until 2 000 dwarfs are produced
in this vast laboratory
where their learned scientists
leisurely study
these fascist-made cripples
We are the living victims
of Zyklon B and Gas V
burning from the products of Sasol
imported with deadly love
from Hitler's Germany
Please
WE DEMAND PUNISHMENT

GENOCIDE . . . . DEATHS IN OUR CRADLES
Whose are those born
to die before the age of five?
Whose are those silencing hunger
With water and
more water?
Who is silenced by hunger
forever?
Whose are those pregnant at infancy
whose bloated stomachs
are airspace for disease
which also tire the mind?
Who are those that must have
inferior medical care
paid for from our
starvation wages?

For all those fighting dogs
scavengers in the same garbage dumps
WE DEMAND PUNISHMENT

Someone must pay
for cultural murder
caused by migrant labour!
For families breaking apart
for widows and widowers
in the dawn of life
for socially induced perversions in the compounds
for fatherless parentless children
for Minister of Information
Connie Mulder's famous words
listen once again and let it sink deep in your indictment
"You must understand the African soul
he just loves migrant labour"
WE WANT HIS KIND PUNISHED

They must be judged
they must be punished
for like straws
they bunch and bundle up our people
into Bophuthatswanas of destruction
their divide and
destroy bantustans
to anchor our people on the doldrums of death
in the many hells – seven or ten times seven limbos
of separate and unequal compartments
away from superior
cities and goods we create
WE DEMAND PUNISHMENT

We are hungry
we are diseased
exiled in our motherland
the crime grows
and so does ignorance
caused by capitalist exploitation
using weapons of racism
employing the method of fascism
that is why we will burn
the roots of all our pain
that is why with one voice
we reject non-violence for criminals and
WE DEMAND PUNISHMENT

MAYIBUYE!

POETRY FOR THE PEOPLE | UHLANGAPRESS.CO.ZA

Printed in the United States
By Bookmasters